ENVoY

Your Personal Guide to Classroom Management

By

Michael Grinder

Founder of the ENVoY Trilogy

ENVoY®

Your Personal Guide to Classroom Management

Editors:	Barbara Lawson Patty Kellogg
Illustrator:	Polly Hobbs
Cover design:	Polly Hobbs
Desktop publisher:	Nancy Stout, Stout Graphics FAX: (360) 256-8066

Printed in U.S.A.

ISBN: 978-1-883407-01-8

Library of Congress Catalog Card Number: 93-91575

Copies of *ENVoY*® can be purchased directly from Michael Grinder & Associates, 16303 NE 259th Street, Battle Ground, WA 98604 (360) 687-3238; Fax: (360) 687-0595; www.michaelgrinder.com. Discounts given to volume orders.

To My Mom and Dad

As the song says, "I'm just a living legacy..." of my parents,
for one gave me the zest and audacity to think I have something
to give and the other was a model of a gentle gender.

And to my other folks who believed in Gail and me so much
they financially and emotionally were our umbilical cord as we
made the transition from teaching to "entrepreneuring."

With much love and appreciation.

Michael Grinder

During Michael Grinder's first three years of teaching high school, he observed Carl Rogers modeling that learning occurs in a *safe* atmosphere that comes from forming *relationships*. Working with Sid Simon and Howard Kirschenbaum provided Michael the understanding of how the teacher-student and student-student *relationships* influence the *self-esteem* of all involved. The rich experiences of teaching in Watts, in Escalante's neighborhood of Compton, and on the central Oregon coast with the Siletz Indians taught Grinder that being *well intended* isn't sufficient—we have to be culturally respectful.

After teaching 17 years on three different levels of education, Michael presents to such corporations as Nike, Hewlett-Packard, and Volkswagen. His passion is still in the classroom—in fact, he has personally been in 5,000 classrooms on three continents. His observations have been the basis for two of his five books: *ENVoY* and *Righting the Educational Conveyor Belt* (1989) which details for K-12 teachers a practical understanding of learning styles and especially the makeup of the at-risk population. Dr. Emily Garfield of Stanford and Dr. Jenny Edwards are in the process of publishing the hard data on the effectiveness of the ENVoY Program in schools in several states.

Michael Grinder & Associates is committed to reversing the trend of "over training and under implementing." The ENVoY Program offers a content course, as well as training for district presenters and coaches. There is also an array of offerings for administrators. Check MGA's website for products, services and upcoming conferences and trainings: http://www.michaelgrinder.com

Michael and Gail Grinder live on a tree farm in Washington. They relish time spent with their three grown children, a niece and their families. They feel very blessed that all of them live close by.

Acknowledgment

ENVoY is a detailing of the patterns of excellence in educational non-verbal management. As such, it is not an invention but a noticing. The following is a list of those people who have helped make the detailing possible:

- Judith DeLozier and John Grinder – for mentoring me in how to see and hear.
- Carol Cummings, Robert Garmston, David Lundsgaard, Kate McPherson, Gary Phillips and Dennis Westover – for introducing me to the coaching and educational consultancy model.
- Cheryl Livneh – for her wisdom to encourage coaching and practicum learning.
- Ron Rock – for gently helping me to realize the necessity of hiring a professional editor.
- Patty Kellogg – for taking me beyond just communicating with myself.
- Paula Bramble – our patron saint of computers.
- Thomas Grinder – for teaching me how to have myself represented and still stay home with Gail.
- Richard Anderson, Barbara Lawson, and Diane McIntosh – for pioneering as "resident coaches."
- Polly Hobbs – for the title, illustrations and inspiration.
- Barbara Lawson – for tremendous conceptual revisions and the final reading.
- Kathy Coffin, Janice Sayler and Ruth Vandercook for being readers.
- David Balding, Amy Manning, Marla Ransom, and Val Wilkerson – for assistance with illustrators.
- Cristine Crooks & Gabi Dolke – for conceptual input.
- Joyce Patterson – for providing the music.
- National Training Associates – for sponsoring the national certification of ENVoY practitioners.

To the following national and international sponsors and supporters: Susan Albert, Mary Ellen Brunaugh, Lindagail Campbell, O.J. Cotes, Diana Delich, Carol D'Souza, Henning Eberhagen, Jenny Edwards, David Halstead, Glenda Hutchinson, Bob Lady, Pat Lassanske, Margo Long, Linda McGeachy, Rudolf Schulte-Pelkum, Dr. Lindsey Smith and Marianne Thompson.

And, finally, to Gail Grinder, my personal and professional partner, who kept me on keel so that my enthusiasm for the project was balanced with home and family. Thank you for all those long hours of typing because you believe in our contribution to the world we love—education.

The second edition was greatly assisted by Suzanne Bailey, Ellen Douglass, Kaze Gadway, Amanda Gore, Gail Grinder, Nick Hinebaugh, Polly Hobbs, Michael Lawson, Joyce Patterson, Nancy Stout, Mary Yenik, Kendall Zoller and Steve Zueback.

Table of Contents

Inventions that Change

At Henry Ford Park, located outside Dearborn, Michigan, there is a tribute to Henry Ford's close friend, Thomas Edison. If you were to take a guided tour, you might discover that Edison learned as much from what did not work as he did creating the invention itself. There was no failure for him, only feedback. As the guide leads you through Edison's inventions from the light bulb to the telephone, the tour is often concluded with the question, "What was Edison's most important discovery?"

After Edison's top seven gifts are offered, the group might ask the guide, "Well, what is his proudest contribution?" Surprisingly, the answer is his laboratory, the basis for all of his inventions.

Edison's inventions have significantly changed our perceptions of technology and practices in daily life. Just as Edison's perceptions have changed our daily practices, so can *ENVoY* change your classroom and take you to a new plateau.

Ambassadors

ENVoY has been selected as the title of this work for two reasons: the capital letters E N V Y stand for Educational Non-Verbal Yardsticks; and, secondly, an envoy is like an ambassador who can explain and interpret a culture both to its own members and to those new to that culture.

Mouse

Since we want to decrease our verbal management tendencies in our classrooms and increase attentiveness to our non-verbal messages, a female and male mouse will be our envoys throughout the book. These ambassadors will remind us that effective management is being "quiet as a _ _ _ _ _."

There is a second reason the mouse is our ambassador. When the computer, symbol of the information age, was first introduced, there was general consensus as to its tremendous potential. There was a quick recognition of the need to learn and an equally strong reaction to its lack of usability. The Macintosh®, Windows® and the mouse revolutionized the computer into a user-friendly machine. So, too, ENVoY is our mouse in establishing and/or refining our classroom management skills.

Macintosh® is a registered trademark of the Apple Computer Company.

Windows® is a registered trademark of Microsoft Corporation.

Introduction

*"We are inadvertently in love with the
Influence of Power,
and we need to be in love with the
Power of Influence."*

ENVoY

Educators have always been surrogate parents but now for some students, we are their only adult role model. Increasingly, these students seek attention at any expense. Attention, even if it is negative, is better than no attention at all.

How does this affect the way we manage? More than ever the child needs to have consistent and fair parameters while preserving the relationship between the teacher and student. In the past, a teacher could manage with power to set parameters. An increasing portion of our pupils will not be motivated to behave and learn if we operate with the old authoritarian way of power.

Only if we stop executing from power and start building relationships based on influence can we begin to understand this type of student and find ways to have the pupil both behave and learn. *ENVoY* is based on Influence. It preserves respectful relationships. A master of our art recently remarked,

"Before the students care what you
know, they need to know that you care."

This book extends beyond the classroom to a much broader realm. In our past practices, we have rewarded teachers on the premise that wisdom comes from experience and knowledge. If this were true, then a masters degree makes one a better teacher and university professors are our best communicators. The institutional acceptance of this premise is evidenced in every school district that has a pay scale based on experience and the number of graduate credits earned. However, knowledge is not the same as effective delivery and experience tends to create habits both good and bad. I recently saw a sign that partially summarized *ENVoY*'s paradigm shift,

"Practice doesn't make perfect,
practice makes permanent..."

Delivering

Is our professional experience getting us the permanence we desire? We need to turn our focus beyond the content level of what we teach to the process level of how we deliver the knowledge. The NEA published research indicates that 82% of all teacher's communications are non-verbal messages. Our traditional emphasis has been on the verbal level.

As this applied research shows, the systematic use of non-verbal messages is the single most important skill that any professional uses. By employing the full range of the non-verbal skills found in *ENVoY*, we can learn to manage with finesse and thus nurture the powerful relationships of influence with our students. This book will assist you in two ways: it delineates the strategies for becoming a master of non-verbal management while preserving relationships; and secondly, it embraces collegial professional support.

Collegiality

The professional development pendulum has swung toward collegial coaching. Initially, the contention was that a peer could enter a colleague's classroom to observe, support and offer suggestions, and the teacher would become more competent. In those schools that reached the level where the teachers wanted peer feedback, it seemed that coaching was the vehicle for professional development. Staff members were enthusiastic. However, in time the collegial involvement waned. A closer examination revealed an interesting pattern: the teacher still wanted the input, but the coach shied away from the invitation to observe. We learned that it wasn't the coaching in and of itself that made the difference but the abilities and comfort level of the coach. The abilities are at least twofold: a format for knowledgeable observations and secondly, respectful feedback. Therefore, while the first half of *ENVoY* allows for self observation and reflection, the second half is formatted for structured observation and non-judgemental feedback. *ENVoY* offers a template for respectful and ecological reinforcement of non-verbal management skills.

As the poetic bard might rhetorically ask, "From whence cometh professional wisdom?" The answer is from our collective insightful reflection on experience. We absolutely need to share the wealth that is locked inside our closed-door classrooms... and the way to do it is through voluntary peer-structured observations and non-judgmental feedback. Visiting our colleague's rooms will allow us to see the process forest from the content trees. In your hands is our collective wisdom about classroom management as well as the ability to influence the students through positive relationships. These are the prerequisites for effective teaching.

Oh, by the way, the third line on the sign mentioned earlier that completes the paradigm shift is,

"...perfect practice makes perfect."

Michael & Gail Grinder
Battle Ground, WA USA
July 12, 1993

How To Use ENVoY

Just being aware of applied research about non-verbal communication in the classroom doesn't result in most teachers changing their habits; therefore, *ENVoY* has incorporated the finest format for professional development: practical exercises and peer coaching.

Chapter Organization

There are four phases of a lesson when management techniques are used: Getting Their Attention, Teaching, Transition to Seatwork and Seatwork. Since the reader will copy the individual skillsheets from the book, these skillsheets will be identified by a logo at the bottom of the page coinciding with the particular phase of a lesson that it pertains to.

While there are more than 30 skills associated with these four phases of a lesson, the chapters are organized to move you in a palpable way toward mastery. Each chapter will give an overview of the skills and suggestions as to which level of education the skillsheet applies.

Self Forms

Chapters One through Five include practical exercises. You will know best which ones you want to do several times before moving on to the next skill. Be ambitious enough to realize that a habit is formed by doing a technique between six and twenty times. Fortunately, we have opportunities to do these maneuvers hundreds of times a week.

CHAPTER ONE: This includes the top seven skills from all four phases of a lesson. This will provide you with an immediate improvement in your use of non-verbal classroom communication. Read and do this chapter before any others. They are highlighted by "gem tabs."

CHAPTERS TWO THROUGH FIVE: These chapters elaborate on the non-verbal skills used during the four phases of a lesson. Having completed Chapter One, you can then select chapters in any progression you choose and they will make sense. There are three outstanding skills that are highlighted by gem tabs and by gem icons on the Table of Contents.

Getting Their Attention

Teaching

Transition to Seatwork

Seatwork

Peer Forms

Chapters Six through Ten are the corresponding peer forms for the first five chapters. After you have sufficiently practiced a selected skill, invite a colleague in to observe you doing the skill.

Teaching Levels

Some of the skills are designed for a certain population of educators more than others. Educators in classrooms where the students stay for two or more hours will be interested in the entire *ENVoY*. Tertiary professors and lecturers will be more drawn to those skills pertaining to the first two phases: Getting Their Attention and Teaching. Secondary teachers and specialists will especially appreciate Chapters One through Three and Six through Nine and some aspects of the other chapters.

In addition to these guidelines, certain skills have been written with a given grade level used in the examples. You will recognize how to modify them to your students' needs.

Copyright and Duplication

We ask that you respect the originality of the author and tell any interested educators to purchase their own copies of *ENVoY*. Districts involved with using this template for their staff's professional development are invited to contact Michael Grinder & Associates for a discount on volume purchases. We welcome exploring how to train resident educators in your system to teach and coach others. See Inservice Offerings in the Appendix for details.

Teaching institutes are encouraged to use *ENVoY* as a manual for professional development. Of course, what you model speaks louder than what you recommend your student teachers do. And yet it is also true that a road sign doesn't have to have been to a destination in order to direct someone there.

Legality

The purchaser of this book has full permission to copy and use any and all pages for him or herself. This includes:

- the self forms of Chapters One through Five,

- the peer forms in Chapters Six through Ten that someone else fills out on you, and

- the forms from Chapters Six through Ten that you fill out on a peer. This latter, however, is intended for your practice as an observer only and is not to be in any way shared with the person being observed.

Teachers may read and study school-owned books; however, they are not permitted to duplicate the forms. Only teachers who own their own books may duplicate the forms.

Glossary

At-Risk Students

A term used to describe the quarter of the student population that is susceptible to dropping out. There are two categories of these pupils: those in jeopardy because of psychological and maturation reasons or those who are not visual learners (e.g. kinesthetic, right-brain oriented or too auditory).

Auditory

A descriptive word applying either to a style of teaching or learning. Auditory learners remember what they heard and talked about. Their propensity for unsolicited comments and discussions is seen as troublesome by instructors. They do much better on daily work than on tests because daily work is reinforced in the same sequential order that it was originally presented whereas on tests the information is rearranged.

Break & Breathe

The maneuver at the end of disciplining when you break your body posture at the same time you breathe. This allows teacher and students to have amnesia about the discipline so that all can focus on the pending learning. Follow the break and breathe with a softer and slower voice pattern.

Decontaminating

Sorting the class's mental states by systematically associating them with certain non-verbal attributes (i.e., locations). Example: disciplining in a different part of the room from teaching or sorting professional life from home life.

Decrease - Increase

See *Right-brain Days*

Dissociated

When one is not in touch with his or her feelings. A good strategy for stressful times, especially when disciplining because the teacher is able to determine the appropriate length and vehemence of the management.

Educational Binoculars

The classroom can be viewed with educational binoculars. ENVoY focuses on the management aspects of the learning environment. Equally important is the other educational tube—curriculum. A teacher can only be a successful manager if he or she can manage the student into work where the student is successful.

Exit Directions

These are the instructions given for Seatwork during the Transition to Seatwork. It is recommended that they be listed visually and that those directions used on a routine basis be laminated for quicker posting.

Hemispherology

The study of the functioning of each side of the brain. The left side is logical, sequential, reality-oriented and has internal focus. Students with this preference like to learn by seeing the example on the board and duplicating. This is how school operates. The right side is random, creative, impulsive; it is the style of the kinesthetic students. Students with this style of thinking are more tactile and like to learn by hands-on projects, movement, touch and remember by locations. While the theory of hemispherology is no longer supported by research, it is a useful model to increase teachers' sensitivity to students' motivation, needs and how to respond to them.

Kinesthetic

A descriptive word applying either to a style of teaching or learning. Kinesthetic learners like to learn by movement and touch. School is often too static for them. They love entertainment and are very self-selective. They are the students most often disciplined by teachers.

Influence Approach

A style of managing in which the teacher INDIRECTLY approaches the inappropriate student. This often involves approaching from the side with eyes directed on the student's work. The teacher has relaxed breathing and doesn't stand as physically close to the student as in the direct approach. The value of this approach is that the student is more likely to go *on task*. The student tends to believe that he is complying because he wants to. This approach preserves the relationship between the teacher and the student. Education desperately needs to incorporate this approach.

Left-brain Student

See *"Hemispherology"*

NEA

National Education Association, the USA's largest teachers' organization. The association publishes researchers' findings such as the fact that 82% of all teacher com-

munications are non-verbal messages (Patrick Miller from "Nonverbal Communication," one booklet in the series, *What Research Says to the Teacher*, Washington D.C.: National Education Association, 1981).

Negative Reinforcement

When teachers correct students for inappropriate behavior, the students, in essence, get contact. Pupils who don't have enough adult contact at home unwittingly seek any contact, even negative contact. The teacher inadvertently is reinforcing negative behavior. This is often the liability of the *Power Approach*.

NLP

Neuro Linguistic Programming - an approach to communication developed by John Grinder and Richard Bandler. It was based on a psychological model. NLP was initially taught as a set of assumptions and skills primarily for a one-on-one setting. Educational NLP is a set of patterns that is used by effective educators; it is geared for the group setting of a classroom. *ENVoY* is one of several books that delineates these patterns.

Power Approach

A style of managing in which the teacher DIRECTLY approaches the inappropriate student. This often involves the teacher approaching the student from the front with eye contact. The teacher is breathing high in a stressful manner and is physically close to the student. The liability of this approach is that the student often only goes from *off task* to *neutral* rather than *on task*. The student complies because of the teacher and *Negative Reinforcement* occurs. In order to preserve the relationship between the teacher and student, education needs to replace this approach with the *Influence Approach.*

Right-brain Days

Those days when the routines are broken and students act more kinesthetic. These days typically include the week before winter vacation, picture day, the first day of snow, etc. On these days, the teacher will want to *decrease* reliance on the instructor, lecture, new material, authority and critical thinking and, at the same time, *increase* group dynamics, use of manipulatives, review material and rapport. Sometimes the morning could be used for left-brain activities and after lunch might be a "surprise right-brain afternoon."

Right-brain Students

See *"Hemispherology"*

Vacuum Pause

That instant when the student finishes focusing on one thing and before he focuses on the next thing. The student is in a limbo state; he is in a temporary "neutral."

Visual

A descriptive word applying either to a style of teaching or learning. Visual learners have the easiest time in school. They learn by remembering what they see. They have the ability to rearrange information; this is the skill necessary to do well on tests. They tend to think methodically and quickly. Visual teaching includes being neat and orderly, showing content on the board or overhead, modeling how to do something, etc.

Visual Atmosphere

When the room is productive. This term is especially applied to the Seatwork phase of the lesson. It is a result of the teacher being visual with directions and doing the non-verbal behaviors that foster concentration: pausing after all announcements, using a lower voice when assisting students, walking around the room slowly and quietly and using minimal verbal and maximum non-verbal communication.

Mouse Doodles

Be ambitious enough to be patient.
Practice one skill a week.

Radar was first conceived in 1904. How long before it was actually realized?

THE 7 GEMS
from the
FOUR PHASES

Chapter One: The Seven Gems

*"The right word may be effective but no word was ever
as effective as the right timed pause."*

Mark Twain

This is the collection of the top seven skills for improving your techniques during the four phases of a lesson: Getting Their Attention, Teaching, Transition to Seatwork and Seatwork. Only when you have them on a habitual level are you then able to profit from other selections of the book. In fact, some users of this manual will be more than satisfied just to have learned these competencies.

When To Use

It's possible that as you read about these skills you will be tempted to say, "That's simple!" Be wary in education of only the cognitive level of understanding. It is the booby prize; otherwise, why aren't the Ph.D.s of the tertiary level the best classroom communicators? You don't need any of these non-verbal skills when you have an easy class or on days when you are *ON*. In fact, you only consciously need these skills in two situations: the first occurs on days when you are having a rough day and are OFF so you will know how to get back ON. That is why ENVoY's format is to have you try the least recommended way of doing a non-verbal skill and then the suggested methodology. This will have two benefits: "self discovery" and the realization about what is an *OFF* day vs. an *ON* day. The former is when your non-verbal responses are a result of being in stress. The latter occurs when we use the non-verbal communication of *ENVoY*. The sec-

ond occasion when you need to consciously know these techniques is when you are trying to mentor someone else. It is a common cry among master teachers when responding to our doting practicum students who are appropriately asking a zillion questions to say, "I'm not sure how or why I did that today! I'm sorry I can't explain myself better."

Mechanics

The titles of the seven most effective skills used during the four phases of a lesson are in italics and listed under the phase in which they belong.

These icons appear on the bottom of worksheets to indicate which phase of the lesson the skill belongs to. The icons are pictured here in a circular fashion to indicate how, as teachers, we rotate through them over and over.

Mouse Doodle

You are encouraged to be patient. That is why the Mouse Doodle pages ask you to reflect on the patience that was required to bring a concept into fruition.

The power of how The Seven Gems can influence you or, more correctly, influence your students will become evident as you learn and practice these two fundamental ENVoY principles:

> · The systematic use of non-verbal signals is the essence of masterful communication.
>
> · The single most powerful non-verbal skill is the P A U S E.

Since *ENVoY* is used as a text and workbook for university courses, the top of the skillsheets have a place for the participant's name.

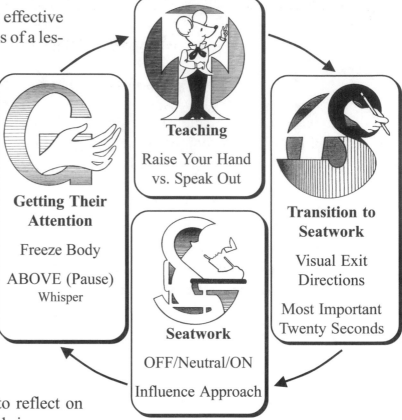

Getting Their Attention

Freeze Body

ABOVE (Pause)
Whisper

Teaching

Raise Your Hand vs. Speak Out

Transition to Seatwork

Visual Exit Directions

Most Important Twenty Seconds

Seatwork

OFF/Neutral/ON

Influence Approach

Gender Reference

As an author, my desire is to facilitate an ease in reading and yet be respectful of gender. Efforts have been made to use "teacher" and "student" wherever possible, and yet there are places that the politics of "he" and "she" surface. In Getting Their Attention and Transition to Seatwork, the teacher is referred to by the male pronoun and the student with the female pronoun. In Teaching and Seatwork, the teacher is referred to with the female pronoun and the student with the male pronoun.

Mouse Doodles

Be ambitious enough to be patient.
Practice one skill a week.

Radar was finally realized in 1939 — 35 years after it was first conceived. The zipper was first conceived in 1883. How long before it was actually realized?

Freeze Body

Least Recommended

Recommended

A local, highly respected University professor stated, "As much as we may resent it, we are blessed to have ESL students because it forces us to 'do as we say.' Instead of telling the class to take out a pen and paper, we have to hold up a pen and paper. Likewise, if we want them to stop what they are doing, we have to stop moving also."

Freeze Body

The opening of a lesson is a critical time because the tone and expectations are established; therefore, effective communication is essential. The traditional way of getting the class' attention is for the teacher to indicate that it's time to begin. The actual wording varies based on grade level and individual instructor's style: "Class," "May I have your attention," "Folks," "Gang," "Year four," "Freeze," etc. All of these verbally communicate, "STOP and focus up here."

The instructor's non-verbal techniques that support the verbal level of Getting Their Attention are the following:

- standing still (hence the title of this skill)

- being in the front of the room (the location of authority and associated with students' attentiveness)

- toes pointed ahead

- weight on both feet

- giving oral directions that are brief

What happens when there is a discrepancy between the teacher's verbal message of STOP and the teacher's non-verbal communication of MOVE? As you ask them to STOP what they are doing, they will look up. If you are walking, they notice that you are non-verbally contradicting yourself by continuing to MOVE, so they tend to go back to what they were previously doing. This is especially true when you are assisting students during seatwork and you realize that you need their attention to further clarify a concept. You may feel you are behind on content and therefore are doing what you

consider to be the fastest way of getting their attention, which is moving toward the front of the room while trying to get their attention verbally.

This skill will focus on non-verbally standing still or doing *Freeze Body* while verbally asking the class members for their attention. Research shows the non-verbal communication is more powerful. The following format will allow you to test out how true this contention is in your classroom. The other skills will be addressed in *Freeze Body Refinements*.

Your name _____

Freeze Body

1. List your favorite saying that indicates you want the students' attention:

_____

_____

_____

_____

_____

Least Recommended

2. For two days use this same favorite saying while moving your body. Describe the class' reaction: _____

_____

_____

_____

_____

Recommended

3. Now for two days use the same saying, but this time freeze your body while saying it. When you are helping with their seatwork and you need to give the students some information, you might have the urge to use your favorite saying while moving toward the front. Remember to walk to the front in silence, freeze your body and then get their attention. Describe the difference between what happens during these two days compared to the first two days: _____

_____

_____

_____

_____

_____

Mouse Doodles

Be ambitious enough to be patient.
Practice one skill a week.

The zipper came into fruition in 1913 — 30 years after it was first conceived. Instant coffee was first conceived in 1934. How long before it was actually realized?

ABOVE (Pause) Whisper

There are a variety of ways to get a class' attention. One of the most common means is to simply say, "Class, may I have your attention?" You want the volume of your voice to be slightly ABOVE the class' collective volume.

Whatever your style is, once you have their attention (p a u s e); then drop your voice to a whisper.

Your name _____

ABOVE (Pause) Whisper

There are a variety of ways to get a class' attention. Some of the methods are best suited to a specific grade level. For example, a third-grade teacher can do a clapping maneuver which would never work in ninth grade. One of the most common means is to simply say, "Class, may I have your attention?" You want the volume of your voice to be slightly *ABOVE* the class' collective volume. Whatever your style is, once you have their attention *(P a u s e)*; then drop your voice to a **whisper**.

The above process produces or increases an atmosphere that is quiet, receptive, and productive. Put a sign up on your back wall reading: *ABOVE (Pause) Whisper*.

Drop Voice

1. Date: _____ Time: _____ Any unusual circumstances: _____

_____

2. Description of how you got their attention: _____

_____

_____

3. Guess how long you paused: _____ seconds. How did you know how long to wait?

_____

_____

4. How much lower was your voice when you started to talk and how long was it before you returned to your regular voice? _____

_____

_____

5. Description of results: _____

_____

ABOVE (Pause) Whisper

Worst Day Scenario

What if the students won't respond to the above wording? What about the class that is loud (on right-brain days such as the week before winter vacation)? How do you make the transition if they won't respond?

The volume of a room collectively can be understood and calibrated. By using your voice just above the volume of the class and doing so quickly, your voice will shock or interrupt the class. They will be more outside themselves and more likely to hear.

Having paced ahead of the class' volume, you have reached a very powerful point. At this point, you have a very short time span to lead them into content. You have two effective choices.

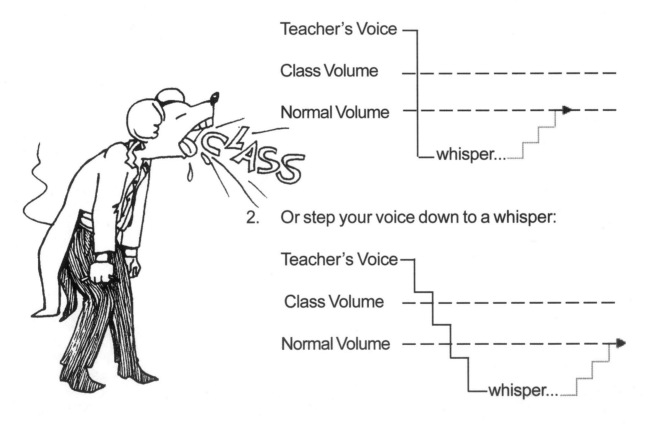

1. Drop your voice to a whisper:

   Teacher's Voice
   Class Volume
   Normal Volume
   whisper...

2. Or step your voice down to a whisper:

   Teacher's Voice
   Class Volume
   Normal Volume
   whisper...

Your name _____

ABOVE (Pause) Whisper

If you have enough auditory voice control, you can do a step-down. The step-down in some cases is your only salvation, but the skill takes more discipline and control to remember to bring your voice volume all the way down to and through the normal range and then down to a *whisper*. The drop to a *whisper* will, for most teachers, be very successful. In either case, either by a direct drop to a whisper or a step-down, make sure you elongate your sentences, slow your voice down and give it a softer timbre. You will put the class in a more listening mode.

If number 1 and number 2 on the previous pages are the effective choices, what do teachers do when they are ineffective? We do one of two things: either don't pause between the *ABOVE* portion (e.g., "Class...") and our content message (e.g., "Turn to page 32. We will be reviewing for tomorrow's test.") or we keep our voice loud as we deliver our content message. This is especially true of physical education teachers and athletic coaches. Of course, the worst maneuver we could do is when we don't pause and keep our voice loud.

Pause → then go low

Step Down Voice

1. Describe the day and approximate time when the class noise level was such that calmly asking for their attention would not have been very effective. _____

_____

2. Use the sharp voice that is slightly above the class' volume and then drop to a *whisper*. List the results here. _____

_____

_____

3. Pick another time when calmly asking for their attention would not be very effective; record the day and the time. _____

_____

4. Use the sharp voice that is slightly above the class' volume and then, step-by-step, lower your voice to and through the normal range and then drop to the *whisper* level.

_____

_____

5. Describe which technique tends to fit your style better and the results you've achieved with either of them. _____

_____

_____

Raise Your Hand vs. Speak Out

From time immemorial, we have been taught that, "A picture is worth a thousand words." The students do what we do more than what we tell them to do!

Raise Your Hand vs. Speak Out

During the teaching portion of a lesson, the educator selects whether she wants to convey information to the class through lecture or have the class be interactive with the instructor. The interaction can be in two forms: the pupils can speak out their answers or they can raise their hands and wait to be recognized before responding. In summary, there are three modes or formats of teaching or presenting material:

Teacher Only One Talking

Raise Your Hand

Speak Out

Each mode has certain functions and characteristics.

Teacher Only One Talking

The instructor can cover more content and often has more control.

Speak Out

This method has the potential to generate the most enthusiasm, and yet the energy level of the students can be volatile enough to be troublesome in terms of classroom control.

Raise Your Hand

This is somewhat between the other two modes. The control is better than Speak Out and yet less than Teacher Only One Talking. Likewise the enthusiasm is greater than Teacher Only One Talking and yet less than Speak Out. Besides being a blend of the other two formats, Raise Your Hand has the distinct advantage of allowing the teacher to monitor the thinking of individual students.

How? Teacher Only One Talking doesn't provide the opportunity for the teacher to know if certain students are comprehending. Speak Out is such a fine involving activity that when the teacher asks the question, the quicker-thinking students tend to dominate. By employing the Raise Your Hand format, the instructor governs the length of time before the answer is given. This increases the "wait time," which has the effect of more students having the necessary time to think and thereby Raise their Hands. The teacher then knows which students comprehend.

Three Ways of Reinforcing the Formats

There are three ways each of the three modes or formats can be activated or sustained:

- Verbally—the teacher can verbally indicate which format is in operation.

- Non-verbally—the teacher can indicate the format through gestures.

- Momentum—The law of inertia states that an object in motion tends to remain in motion and if it is still it tends to remain still. In other words "momentum." Applying this principle to the three formats means that once a format has been used for a certain length of time (either enforced verbally or non-verbally or both) the format will tend to remain even if the verbal and non-verbal levels are dropped.

Raise Your Hand vs. Speak Out

A diagram of the three formats and levels would look like this:

FORMATS:	Teacher Only One Talking	Raise Your Hand	Speak Out
LEVELS:			
Verbal:	"Listen up." "My turn."	"Raise your hand if..."	"Everyone."
Non-Verbal:	teacher pointing to self, hand in a traffic cop gesture of a "stop sign."	teacher models by raising her hand.	teacher gestures from class back toward self.
Momentum:	(This occurs once the teacher has done the same format for several consecutive times.)		

Safest Method

The *safest method* of establishing a format is to use both the verbal level and, simultaneously, model with a gesture. Every time you switch to a new mode, consider doing the verbal and non-verbal messages together.

Better Maneuver

The *better maneuver* is to initially do both the verbal and non-verbal level together for at least two consecutive times, then drop the verbal level and do the non-verbal signal only. The non-verbal level has many by-products: the room is quieter, the students become more visual, the students are watching the teacher more and the teacher's voice is reserved for either content or positive reinforcement.

Ultimate Technique

The *ultimate technique* is progressing from the verbal and non-verbal level (Safest Method) through the non-verbal level alone (*Better Maneuver*) to dropping the non-verbal signal also and noticing that most of the time the class will keep the momentum and still remain in the current operating mode.

Be Sensitive When

Especially *be sensitive* to *when* you switch from the Speak Out mode; drop your voice and hold still when you initiate the Teacher Only One Talking or Raise Your Hand. In other words, using the diagram at the top of the page, you are OK when moving from columns in a left to right fashion but need to be cautious when going from the right to left direction.

Your name_____

Raise Your Hand vs. Speak Out

Taking Inventory

For two days create verbal directions and non-verbal gestures for each of the three modes. If you already have wording and non-verbal messages, notice what they are. List the verbal and non-verbal communication below.

Teacher Only One Talking: _____

_____

_____

Raise Your Hand: _____

_____

Speak Out: _____

_____

_____

Usually during the Teaching portion of a lesson each teacher will have a certain mode(s) that she tends to do more than the other two. What was the mode that you used more than others? One way to determine this is to have yourself or someone else tally by 1-3 minute intervals which mode was used the most:

Date:_____ Starting time of tally:_____ Ending time of tally: _____

Length of intervals: _____ minutes

Teacher Alone	**Raise Your Hand**	**Speak Out**
_____	_____	_____

Which one is your favorite? _____

Is this typical or were there any unusual circumstances: _____

_____

_____

Notice if there is a particular pattern or sequence that you habitually use. Sometimes a teacher will open with a Teacher Only One Talking to do presentation and then will switch to Raise Your Hand in order to monitor the students' understanding and release the class to do seatwork. Other times an instructor will open the lesson by having the students reflect and share about something that they have already experienced so that the teacher can teach from the "known to the unknown." Your pattern or sequence of modes may be based on the particular content you are covering. Therefore, list a couple of your patterns and mention when you use each.

Your name_____

Raise Your Hand vs. Speak Out

Sequence of modes and when utilized: _____

_____

_____

Another sequence of modes and when utilized: _____

_____

_____

Strategies

The Safest Method

For a full day or more employ both the verbal and non-verbal messages every time you initiate each of the modes. Date of implementation: _____

Describe how the results are different from what used to occur:

Teacher Only One Talking: _____

_____

Raise Your Hand: _____

_____

Speak Out: _____

_____

The Better Maneuver

For a full day or more, do the verbal and non-verbal messages when you initiate a mode. Then after doing both the verbal and non-verbal messages two or three times, drop the verbal and do just the non-verbal message. Date of implementation: _____
Describe how long the verbal and non-verbal messages had to be used together before you were able to drop the verbal and do just the non-verbal communication:

Teacher Only One Talking: _____

_____

Raise Your Hand: _____

_____

Speak Out: _____

Your name _____

Raise Your Hand vs. Speak Out

Strategies

The Ultimate Technique

For a full day or more, do the verbal and non-verbal communications together, then drop the verbal level and then drop the non-verbal messages. Date of implementation: _____ Describe how long you had to do the non-verbal gesture alone before you could drop it and the class would maintain the momentum and still do the same mode:

Teacher Only One Talking: _____

_____

Raise Your Hand: _____

_____

Speak Out: _____

_____

Be Sensitive When

The sequence that most educators report as the most dangerous is when the instructor switches from more to less student involvement. For the majority of teachers, the most volatile sequence is to move from Speak Out to Teacher Only One Talking. And progressively easier is from Speak Out to Raise Your Hand and Raise Your Hand to Teacher Only One Talking. When the instructor switches from more to less student involvement, the suggestion is that the teacher drops her voice and stands still. Which is your most volatile sequence? Try these suggestions and report how they assisted:

_____

_____

_____

_____

_____

_____

_____

Exit Directions

Visual Information Empowers

One of the major indicators that our society is shifting from the world of "power" to a world of "influence" is the increasing use of the term "empowerment." When we orally give directions, we inadvertently shackle the students to us because we are the only ones with the accurate information. We have to visually display information. Visual information empowers people because they are independent of the source of the information. Before the printing press, the world was dependent on those individuals who had knowledge. The publication of books freed people to be independent. So, we too want to do this with our students.

This is the single most important skill of the whole book. All the other skills of the Transition and the Seatwork phases depend on the *Exit Directions* being displayed visually.

Exit Directions

The elementary and secondary level lessons are usually composed of lecture or presentation, directions for seatwork and then the actual seatwork. Some secondary and most tertiary levels have class time spent in a presentation format which often ends with suggested or required homework. For all three levels of education, the directions given at the end of the presentation signal a decrease in the availability of the teacher. Therefore we will term these directions as *Exit Directions*. These *Exit Directions* usually involve between one and three items. The elementary level, which is self-contained, might have the following *Exit Directions*:

"Finish your math assignment on page 65, problems one through ten. Show all of your work. It is due today. Then work on your spelling; Chapter 20 is due this Friday. If you finish it, you can have free reading."

The secondary level is more likely to be organized on a rotating system with each subject taught by a separate teacher. An example of the *Exit Directions* on this level might be:

"The assignment for tonight is page 65, the end of the chapter questions one through ten. Write out your answers in full sentences. They are due at the start of the period tomorrow. Remember the big test is this Friday. It is worth twenty-five percent of this quarter's final grade. You would be smart to understand the concepts of ...."

Confusing

The above examples indicate the complexity of *Exit Directions*. Most students clearly understand each separate aspect of the directions. What they find overwhelming is the amount of information and, more importantly, that the directions are given orally. Evidence of how *confusing* the oral format of giving *Exit Directions* can be is demonstrated by the frequent stream of students coming up to the teacher and trying to find out specific details. The bewildered pupils often preface their queries with, "Did you say...?" or "In other words, you want us...?" or "Let me see if I have this right; we are to do...?" At times, it is a particular aspect such as, "Where do we put this when we finish...?" Sometimes we feel like screaming the answer because the information the student is seeking is so obvious to us. This is especially true when the instructor has used the same routines since the start of the year. Someone once said, "Teachers are seasonal workers whose tongues get tired and wear out before any other part of their body." The cause of our frustrations and the students' is that it is difficult to remember so much information using only listening skills.

Your name _____

Exit Directions

The solution is to write the *Exit Directions* on the board so that there is a stable visual representation of what we said. Visual *Exit Directions* both increase the clarity of the message and double the length of the memory. This, of course, frees the teacher from having to be a parrot repeating what was said. The instructor can now assist students one-on-one during the **Seatwork** segment of the lesson.

1. Write out a typical sample of your *Exit Directions*. Make sure you can satisfy a Philadelphia lawyer as to what is to be done, how it is to be done, when it is due and where it is to be put when done. And, most importantly, include what the student is to do when finished.

_____

_____

_____

_____

Employing Non-verbal Signals

2. The best way for students to know which, of all the information on the board, are the *Exit Directions* is to be systematic in terms of where (location) and how (color of chalk used and writing style) they are listed. Some self-contained classroom teachers use different colors for different subjects, e.g., math is blue. One smart fourth-grade instructor puts a rubber stamp print on the back of the kinesthetic students' hands as they leave at the end of the day so that when the students get home they have a reminder of homework that needs to be done. The ink pad color matches the subject's color, e.g., English is green. Describe the non-verbal methods you will be using so that even a student who has been daydreaming and has returned to earth would know which, of all the information on the board, are the *Exit Directions*: _____

_____

_____

Your name _____

Exit Directions

Lamination

3. Teachers don't have time to fully write out the information stated in number one on the previous page. A suggestion is to write out the information that is used on a regular basis on tag board and then laminate the tag board. Sometimes the same information is used in the same manner over and over. Other times you will want to leave blanks on the card where, using an erasable overhead transparency pen, you can put the specific information for that particular day. The example used on page 29 is duplicated below followed by the laminated version in the shadow boxes. If there is more than one content area involved, then use a separate card for each.*

"Finish your math assignment on page 65, questions one through ten. Show all your work. It is due today.

Then work on your spelling; Chapter 20 is due this Friday.

If you finish it, you can have free reading."

*Math page:*_____ *#:*_____ *Due:* _____
Conditions: _____

*Spelling, Chapter:*_____ *Due:* _____
Conditions: _____

Translate your *Exit Directions* stated in number 1 on the previous page in the format used for lamination: _____

_____

_____

_____

_____

_____

*Samples can be downloaded from www.michaelgrinder.com.

Most Important Twenty Seconds

Auditory Students

MITS stands for the *Most Important Twenty Seconds* of any lesson. By standing still for twenty seconds after releasing the class to do **Seatwork**, more students will go ON task independently.

There is a subtle by-product that the MITS produces. Every classroom has one to five students who need to repeat our *Exit Directions* to us. They are our auditory students. Their brains are like a cassette player—when they hear our voices saying the directions, they want to record the message in their own voice—so they come up and say the same thing we just said. As instructors we are confused.

By doing the MITS when the auditory student comes up to us, we non-verbally signal him to return to his seat. When the twenty seconds is finished, we then approach that pupil. Often the student is fine and doesn't need us. We are really assisting the auditory learner by helping him learn to internally talk to himself instead of doing the transcription aloud. This is a skill that will put him in good stead with his future working colleagues—the educated workforce doesn't respect the person who, in order to think, has to clarify aloud.

Your name_____

Most Important Twenty Seconds

When the teacher finishes direct instruction and the students are about to begin their seatwork, a transition is being made from group-oriented to one-on-one help. This transition is best done through a combination of visual *Exit Directions* and by modeling your expectations that they will be concentrating. The most productive seatwork atmosphere, whether it is the students working alone or with partners (e.g., cooperative learning), is a visual one...meaning purposeful, often silent but not necessarily so. Suggestions on how to model this visual atmosphere are the following:

1. Read the *Exit Directions*.

2. Ask if there are any questions. Answer them orally as you write the additional answers or information on the board.

3. Release the students with wording such as, "You may begin now."

4. **Most Important Twenty Seconds** (MITS): freeze your body and wait 20 seconds while you model for the students how quiet and concentrating you would like them to be. If students are requesting help by raising their hands or speaking out, keep your eyes scanning the room, visually stay very still and, with hand gestures, indicate to those students that you will be with them in a second. Some elementary teachers have a Hula Hoop® that they stand in during this MITS. The kinesthetic learners who are seeking help can see the physical hoop and therefore are reminded in a concrete way that the teacher is not yet available.

5. Slowly move to help the students individually.

One major by-product of this technique that teachers appreciate is that the students who often come up to us and ask us to repeat the information will learn to do this internally during the twenty seconds. This saves us time and makes them more independent. You will need to modify the length of time based on the grade level. For second graders, you can only wait ten seconds.

Instructions: Using the format on number one through five above, list how this approach worked. To cement this habit both for you and the class, make this technique your main focus for a week. By then, you will want to do it automatically. Circle the day as you practice the skill.

Week from _____ to _____

M T W Th F 1. Read visual *Exit Directions*.

M T W Th F 2. Ask for questions and write as you orally answer.

M T W Th F 3. Release the students by saying _____

_____

M T W Th F 4. Stay still and be patient during the *MITS*.

M T W Th F 5. Slowly go help students individually.

List your results: _____

OFF/Neutral/ON

Gail and I think the book should be dedicated to our dogs because the foundation and power of all the ENVoY skills could be experienced by successfully training a puppy:

- systematic use of non-verbal communication
- the power of the pause
- getting their attention before giving a message
- catch 'em doing it right, then reinforce

OFF/Neutral/ON is a concept that is designed specifically for one-on-one situations. Take your time training yourself. When the training is consistent, we have much greater success with the individual student.

OFF/Neutral/ON

The kinesthetic student often has a high degree of distractibility during seatwork and may need one-on-one attention to stay on task. As a result, teachers often feel like they need to stand next to the student in order for the student to remain productive. Usually a classroom has two to six students who fit such a description. On some days a teacher has to literally race from one of these students to the next putting them back on task. On the surface it looks like this type of student is either *ON task* or *OFF task*, but a closer examination reveals that there is a third mental state in between the two that we will label *Neutral*. This is important because as the teacher races around with octopus arms putting off-task students back on task, that instructor is probably just putting them from OFF to Neutral. It is like the gears of a car; we really don't shift from one mental state/gear to another without going through neutral.

Through trial and error, instructors have learned that kinesthetic students often don't hear or see well so that teachers have to touch them or, at the very least, be near them to get their attention. By the time certain students reach fourth grade, they respond to a teacher's presence with guilt. This reminds me of an anecdote which, based on the description, must have involved a kinesthetic person. One stormy night, a large branch from a huge tree in the yard crashes through the upstairs window. Mom, asleep downstairs, is awakened and immediately concerned about the safety of her son who sleeps upstairs. She yells out, "Eli!" Eli immediately responds with, "Mom, it wasn't me this time!"

What do "at risk" students do when the teacher approaches? They hold their breath! The following inadvertent scenario often occurs:

a. Student off task   = OFF

b. Teacher approaches

c. Student holds breath   = Neutral

d. Teacher leaves

e. Student finally breathes
    and goes back off task   = OFF

Your name _____

OFF/Neutral/ON

1. It is strongly recommended that you select only two students to do this with and concentrate on doing this for a minimum of two or three weeks. Since you are learning a new process skill, don't select your two "worst case students." It is much better for you to select marginal students because you will be able to perfect your timing. Later you can apply these techniques to the more distractible or difficult students.

First student's initials: _____   Second student's initials: _____

Least Recommended

2. For a given seatwork time period, intentionally approach these students in a rushed and punitive manner. Notice if they tend to hold their breath. Then move away from them and see if they tend to go back off task once you leave. Describe what happens.

_____   _____

_____   _____

_____   _____

_____   _____

_____   _____

Recommended

3. During this same seatwork time period, approach them in a slow manner and stay until they finally breathe and go back on task, then slowly leave. It is highly recommended that you move away from behind them so they don't know when you actually leave. Describe your speed of approach, how long you stayed, how you could see they were breathing and on task, how you slowly left them, and, of course, the results:

_____   _____

_____   _____

_____   _____

_____   _____

_____   _____

Mouse Doodles

Be ambitious enough to be patient.
Practice one skill a week.

Instant Coffee was finally realized in 1956 — 22 years after it was first conceived. Photography was first conceived in 1782. How long before it was actually realized?

Influence Approach

The Power Approach

The Influence Approach

My Uncle K. Nine always likes to say there are two ways to train a puppy to sit. We can push the dog's rump down and say the word, "Sit!" Or we can run the pooch around the block and as the puppy tires and starts to sit down we say, "Sit!" Sometimes the difference between power and influence is timing.

Influence Approach

It is IMPERATIVE that you have completed the *OFF/Neutral/ON* skillsheet before you begin this. The skills mentioned in previous sections are further refined by understanding the difference between the Power Approach and the *Influence Approach*.

POWER Approach	INFLUENCE Approach
1. Teacher approaches from the front.	Teacher approaches from the side.
2. Teacher's eyes on student's face.	Teacher's eyes on student's work.
3. Teacher isn't breathing.	Teacher is breathing.
4. Teacher is close to student.	Teacher is farther from the student.
5. Teacher waits until student is in Neutral.	Teacher waits until student is ON task. ON task.

{Number five is what pages 35 - 36 of *OFF/Neutral/ON* are about.}

Knowing that there are more ingredients than just the above differences, one possible way to summarize the above is to say POWER IS DIRECT and INFLUENCE IS INDIRECT.

The teacher who uses Power gives the sense of feeling personally threatened by the student and consequently, the intervention is "confrontational." The instructor using *Influence* is separating the student as a person from the student's behavior. The focus is on the work.

Does the Power Approach work? In many cases it does because there is an increasing number of students who don't have a lot of human contact with adults at home. We know that students much prefer to have positive contact, but their second preference is to have any contact rather than no contact. This population of students is unconsciously willing to get in trouble in order to have adult contact. A poet once said, "Children will get our attention; the question of whether it is positive or negative is based on how soon and often we give it." The *Influence* technique is designed to break the "negative reinforcement syndrome." The liability of the Power Approach is that the teacher has to physically remain to have the student comply. There is no self-motivation.

How would a teacher increase her influence on a student being ON task during seatwork? Since it is often the teacher's proximity to the kinesthetic student that puts that student ON task, the teacher could move into the student's area indirectly. The farther the instructor is from the student and yet is still able to manage, the more the student tends to believe that he is ON task because of his efforts instead of the teacher's presence. This truly is *INFLUENCE*.

Your name _____

Influence Approach

Once the student is ON task and has taken two breaths, then the teacher can approach the student.

The steps to implement the *Influence Approach* include:

1. Move toward the student without looking at the student (e.g., have the student be 45 degrees off from the front of your face) until the student shifts from OFF to at least Neutral.

2. PAUSE.

3. You are looking at an adjacent student's work while peripherally watching the targeted student. What are you watching for? You want to see if the students goes from Neutral to ON task. Wait until he breathes because when that happens, the student will tend to move from Neutral to ON task. If the student starts to go back OFF, immediately move closer. If the *Influence Approach* is not sufficient to result in ON-task behavior, you may want to temporarily add some of the elements of the Power Approach. For instance, you could look directly at the student. If that is not enough, then say his name.

4. Once the student is ON task and has taken two breaths, then go to the student's side. At this point the teacher has many choices: to talk or not, to make eye contact or just look at the work, etc. The choice is based on how to best change "negative reinforcement syndrome" into a "positive contact;" from Power to *Influence*. Use this axiom when experimenting.

Timing

Select two students with whom you want to practice this technique. To increase your chance of success, remember that it is easier to learn a new skill with a "marginal student" than the "worst case scenario" student. It takes more *timing* with the latter group.

Your name _____

Influence Approach

First student's initials: _____   Second student's initials: _____

1. Approach the student indirectly. How far away from the student were you when the student switched from OFF to at least Neutral?

   _____   _____
   _____   _____
   _____   _____

2. Describe what you saw that indicated that the student was going from OFF to Neutral (if possible, mention the student's breathing pattern):

   _____   _____
   _____   _____
   _____   _____

3. You have waited until the student breathed. If he went from Neutral toward OFF, describe what you did:

   _____   _____
   _____   _____
   _____   _____

4. The student has been ON task and has breathed twice. Describe what choice you made and how the goal of "positive contact" was increased:

   _____   _____
   _____   _____
   _____   _____

Getting their attention

Chapter Two: Getting Their Attention

"No one who examines classroom life carefully can fail to be astounded by the proportion of the students' time that is taken up just in waiting."

Charles E. Silberman

Getting a class under way is much like having a ship leave a dock—the better the timing with the ebb and flow, the easier the voyage. Our opening minutes, indeed seconds, convey our level of organization and expectations. Daily we want to set a precedent for the lesson at the start. The two most powerful skills in getting the class' attention so that you can start are *Freeze Body* and *ABOVE (Pause) Whisper*. We presume you have done and mastered these skills from Chapter One. The following skillsheets are designed for all levels of educators.

- *Freeze Body Refinements*
- *Incomplete Sentence*
- *Yellow Light*

Of all the skills, the most important stress-management techniques are *Decontaminating the Classroom* and *Break & Breathe*. We know that students are more resilient than the instructors. We need to be much more concerned with the teacher's emotional well-being; we know that the students will bounce back quite quickly. The key to management that is both effective for them and is still healthy for the teachers is to memorize and act in accordance with the axiom, "We are never paid to feel when we manage." You are an actor! By being in control of your feelings, you can allow yourself to externally show a whole range of emotions: upset/disappointed/hurt/angry. You are doing what they need you to do not how you feel.

This ability allows you to have amnesia when you finish and return to your real profession of giving, imparting, etc. Cultivate this "management persona" as different from the real you who is the teacher. You then avoid overkill. "Don't hunt field mice with elephant guns." When we overdramatize we inadvertently sabotage ourselves in the long run. Like the bugs that survive the onslaught of insecticide—we have to increasingly up the amount of the intensity to get the same results. Do yourself a kinesthetic favor and put a sign on your back wall that says "B & B" (as a reminder to *Break & Breathe*).

The section under *Opening Visual Instructions* called "When There Is No Time" is essential on our off days. It settles us down as well as the students. If you are tertiary level, deal with adolescents or teach adult education, the skills you are looking for are most likely found under Getting Their Attention and Teaching.

Gender Reminder

When applicable, the teacher is referred to with the male pronoun and the student with the female pronoun.

Freeze Body Refinements

Some teachers know how to be an educational **E.F.** Hutton.*

*Effective Feet

Freeze Body Refinements

As mentioned in *Freeze Body*, there are several other non-verbal skills that communicate the message of STOP:

> ## Refinement Techniques
> * Being in the front of the room
> * Toes pointed ahead
> * Weight on both feet
> * Brief directions

A short explanation of each of these non-verbal techniques will be made followed by a suggested way of determining which of these are pertinent to your teaching situation.

The front of the room is where most presentations or lectures are done. Therefore, the class is used to being more attentive when the teacher is there compared to when the teacher is out in the rows helping students during seatwork.

Congruency

When a person's toes are pointed ahead and when the weight is on both feet, the Western culture interprets the speaker as being highly congruent. Congruency conveys the message of, "I expect attentiveness!" Because congruency has a self-fulfilling prophecy, the likelihood of the attentiveness occurring greatly increases. When female instructors are wearing dresses or skirts, they are more likely to have one of their feet pointed off to the side (usually toward the direction they just came from). Be sensitive to this tendency. Once you have the class' attention, then you can operate in any style you choose, including fashion model postures.

When the teacher says a long sentence such as, "Class, stop what you are doing and look up here," the length of the sentence tends to make the teacher's voice blend with the general collective noise level in the room. A shorter call for attentiveness is more likely to be distinguished from the rest of the sounds in the room. There are some other positive by-products of the shorter remark. The teacher doesn't exhaust his oxygen and therefore has an easier time switching from the "traffic cop" role of getting their attention to the instructing persona.

Your name _____

Freeze Body Refinements

l.   Determine which of the above non-verbal techniques you want to experiment with: "location," "toes," "weight," and "length." It is your choice of whether you want to tinker with all four at the same time or isolate them. The ones selected are: _____

_____

_____

These are refinement skills of *Freeze Body*. Make sure you hold your body still while doing them so that you can isolate the variable. This will allow you to determine each variable's impact.

Least Recommended

2. For two days, do the selected refinement skills of number 1 in exactly the opposite manner of what is recommended. For example: don't be in the front of the room, have toes pointed to the side, have more weight on one leg than the other (especially put a hand on the hip) and announce your favorite saying (using a long sentence) for getting their attention. Describe the effect on the class' attentiveness: _____

_____

_____

Recommended

3.   Then for two days employ the selected refinements of the non-verbal skills in number 1 in the recommended manner:

- Be in the front of the room

- Have toes pointed straight ahead

- Your weight evenly distributed

- Announce a brief saying for getting their attention

Describe the difference between what happened during these two days compared to the first two days. Since holding your body frozen is found to be the most powerful non-verbal skill, you may find very little effect: _____

_____

_____

_____

_____

Mouse Doodles

Be ambitious enough to be patient.
Practice one skill a week.

Photography was finally realized in 1838—56 years after it was first conceived. The self-winding wrist watch was first conceived in 1923. How long before it was actually realized?

Opening Visual Instructions

Head Start For The Day
If this Rebus represents the
name **SHAKESPEARE**...

what images would you use to "picture"
ERNEST LAWRENCE THAYER?
Draw or write the name of the images you
would use and turn in tomorrow at the
beginning of the period.
BONUS: Who is ELT?

LITERATURE
DRAMA

Harry Wong, the National Teacher of the Year, is a math instructor. He says there is a direct correlation between the time a class is supposed to start and the actual length of time it takes to get underway. The later it is beyond the bell ringing, the more the students clown around.

Thinklers

Thinklers is an exceptional book of "mental warm-ups" that the students see on the overhead/board when they enter your room. See advertisement on pages 274-280.

Opening Visual Instructions

Applied research shows that teachers who teach visually cover more content and, statistically, have more manageable classrooms. Teaching visually is accomplished by showing directions during three different phases of the lesson:

Getting Their Attention

During the Teaching portion

During the Transition section (Exit Directions)

This section will focus on the first of the three. If the board has the directions on what the students are to do when the students enter the room, they can see what to do. This is extremely important because it is a non-verbal message. Non-verbal messages make for a quieter classroom, students have a higher self-esteem and the teacher's energy level is higher.

There are several purposes for the visual instructions. Often teachers will put on the board an academic warm-up activity. Frequently this is a fun-oriented, pencil and paper activity covering previous content: e.g., a review problem for math, copying a new vocabulary term and its definition or asking a high-interest trivia question. The activity has to be within the students' abilities so that they are independent of you. Otherwise it would be "teaching" instead of a "warm-up to teaching."

Besides using the board for academic warm-up activities, another reason is to assist the transition to the first activity. For instance, "Have a pencil and paper out and open your history book to page 127."

Often the same transitions are used on a regular basis. It is very advisable to laminate them with slot(s) left open for the variable portion (such as the actual page number) and use a water soluble transparency marker. This allows the laminated poster to be used over and over with very little teacher time spent preparing it.

Our goal is to have the students non-verbally go into the appropriate mental state by using visual instructions. What is your style of accomplishing this? Would you have the instructions hidden under a pull-down map or on an overhead that is turned off, and after you've greeted them, reveal the instructions? Would you have the instructions shown as the class walks into the room and you're at the door greeting the pupils? Would you have the instructions shown as they enter and you are standing still at the front modeling attention to the board while greeting the pupils?

Since the contention is that the teacher's non-verbal communications are the single most powerful factor in a classroom, the teacher's modeling of attentiveness to the board is essential. To test this, do the opposite: have the instructions on the board and be moving and doing non-relevant talking while the students enter.

If you are a teacher who has done the above correctly for some time, you may not see any difference because of the previously established routine. Remember that on those days when you need additional assistance in having them make the transition into an academic mode (e.g., picture day, week before winter vacation, etc.) make sure you do model.

Your name _____

Opening Visual Instructions

Least Recommended

1. Teacher movement and non-relevant talking while pupils enter sets a different tone. Describe your movement and non-relevant talk: _____

_____

_____

2. Describe the class' reaction to your movement and non-relevant talk: _____

_____

_____

_____

Recommended

3. List the warm-up activity you like to put on the board at the beginning of class: _____

_____

_____

_____

4. Explain how the activity is within the students' abilities and how they can work independently of you: _____

_____

_____

5. In addition to academic warm-ups, *Opening Visual Instructions* ready students for academic learning. List your opening statement that prepared students for instruction: _____

_____

_____

_____

6. Since the teacher's non-verbal communications are the single most powerful factor in the classroom, modeling of attentiveness is essential. Describe your non-verbal greeting of students and directions to the visual instructions: _____

_____

_____

Your name _____

Opening Visual Instructions

When There Is No Time

The previous section describes the best of all worlds when you have time to prepare the visual instructions ahead of time, but sometimes you don't have time. This often happens when we are rushed doing last-minute things like the week before winter vacation and the class especially needs a smooth opening. What would be helpful to do in these circumstances? There are three possible options. If the teacher first gets the class' attention and then turns to write on the board, he runs the risk of losing their at-tentiveness: the instructor's back is to the pupils and writing is slow. What about get-ting their attention and orally giving them transition directions? Oral directions are the least effective approach to getting them to understand what you want them to do. The suggestion is to experiment with the idea of writing the directions on the board, then get-ting their attention and model for them to focus on the board and follow the directions. You may feel the urge to quiet them first. However, waiting until you are ready to pro-ceed allows for greater attention to the task. Remember this is an emergency procedure.

Intentionally be preoccupied as the students come in.

1. What are you doing? _____

2. Feel the urge to quiet them; describe your tension: _____

   _____

Recommended

3. Instead, go to the board and write the instructions (as mentioned earlier, this is where laminated signs are ideal because they are already done). The instructions are:_____

   _____

   _____

4. Now, how do you get their attention? Remember to keep feet still and pause after ver-bally getting their attention. (See *Freeze Body Refinements* for more information).

   _____

   _____

5. Describe how this approach works compared to your normal routine: _____

   _____

   _____

Incomplete Sentences

We know how effective the *ABOVE (Pause) whisper* is. The teacher uses the *ABOVE* technique from the **management** tube of the Educational Binoculars in order to get the class' attention. Then, the teacher can move into the **curriculum** tube. The *Incomplete Sentence* is a disguised form of the *ABOVE* technique because the teacher says loudly a partial content sentence instead of a management sentence. During the ensuing pause, the class quiets. Then the teacher repeats the content in a whispery voice.

Incomplete Sentences

Often teachers' training courses encourage the instructor to have everyone's attention before beginning, yet we know that when we use our voice for the pace of the lesson and our non-verbal signals for management, the students get into the lesson sooner and remember the lesson as content-oriented. So how could we non-verbally get their attention before beginning?

Stragglers

If the content is of high enough interest, we can start the lesson and the students will respond; however, if we suspect the interest will not be high enough, we can use *Incomplete Sentences*. Students who are not watching the teacher but hear an abrupt stoppage in the middle of the initial phrase of the teacher's sentence will tend to freeze and look up. This maneuver allows quick transi-

tion to attentiveness. Some examples are, "AS WE," "LOOKING AT," "NOTICE HOW." As the inattentive students engage you, repeat the sentence in its entirety and continue. Using the skills learned in *ABOVE (Pause) Whisper* say the incomplete sentence above their collective volume and then repeat the sentence in its entirety in a whispery voice. *Incomplete Sentences* are often effective for those "straggler" students who are slower than other pupils to give the instructor their attention.

Incomplete Sentences can be used any time. The ideal time to employ this technique is on right-brain days (e.g., picture day, first snowfall, etc.) because we want to decrease authority and increase rapport. It is best to practice the timing of this technique before the right-brain days arrive.

Your name _____

Incomplete Sentences

- Is this a left-brain day and you want to practice the timing of this skill? _____

  If so, what makes the day left-brain? _____

- Is this a right-brain day and you are employing this skill? _____

  If so, what makes the day right-brain? _____

  List two of your favorite introductory sentences.

  _____

  _____

Speed and Volume

Freeze Body as you do the initial phrase of the sentence in a higher than usual volume and end with an abrupt stop. Continue the *Freeze Body* during the P A U S E. When you repeat the sentence in its entirety, do so in a whisper.

First Example

1. Date and time of doing *Incomplete Sentence*. _____

2. List incomplete phrase. _____

3. Description of your voice volume during incomplete phrase and how still your body was during the phrase and the brief silence that followed. _____

   _____

4. Description of how you moved your body and breathed after you said the *Incomplete Sentence.* _____

   _____

5. Description of the lower volume and slowness of voice speed as the sentence was said in its entirety in a whispery voice. _____

   _____

6. Describe the effect on the class' attentiveness, especially the stragglers. _____

   _____

   _____

Your name _____

Incomplete Sentences

Second Example

1. Date and time of doing *Incomplete Sentence*. _____

2. List incomplete phrase. _____

3. Description of your voice volume during incomplete phrase and how still your body was during the phrase and the brief silence that followed. _____

_____

_____

4. Description of how you moved your body and breathed after you said the *Incomplete Sentence.* _____

_____

_____

5. Description of the lower volume and slowness of voice speed as the sentence was said in its entirety in a whispery voice. _____

_____

_____

6. Describe the effect on the class' attentiveness, especially the stragglers. _____

_____

Sneak Preview

After you have done the skill, *Break and Breathe*, you can add it to your practice of *Incomplete Sentences*.

• *Freeze Body* during initial phrase and the P A U S E.

• As the students quiet down and look at you in silence, simultaneously take a step and *Break and Breathe*.

• Settle your body (sometimes taking a second breath) and say the sentence in its entirety in a whisper.

Positive Comments

"I really like the way Aaron, Hannah and Mitchell hang up their coats and hats."

Your name _____

Positive Comments

Through the third and fourth grade, the students love to be told by their teacher that they're doing well. Therefore, the finest time to do *Positive Comments* is during a transition because the people who are getting the *Positive Comments* become models for those who are "other than appropriate." For example, the teacher says, "Clear your desk and take out your pencil and paper." Very shortly after that, the teacher comments, "I like the way Johnny is doing this. Oh! Row four, all of you students are ready."

After the fourth grade, the *Positive Comments* have to be subtle and sometimes disguised because of the nature of the peer adolescent awareness level of the students. Whether the teacher can say, "I really like how so and so is doing..." is based on whether the teacher and the acknowledged student(s) maintain a good relationship with the class. If the teacher doesn't have as much rapport, then it's less appropriate to use the word "I" and better to do collective praise as opposed to individual or small group praise. For example, some teachers who have strong rapport are able to say vulnerable, positive transition comments such as, "I really appreciate how quickly you're able to get your stuff ready for our lesson."

1. List your grade level: _____

2. Give four examples of how you currently use *Positive Comments* during transition time:

_____

_____

3. What would be some other areas where you could increase, further refine or use the concept of *Positive Comments* during transition time? List them here.

_____

_____

4. At the end of a week of an increase in *Positive Comments*, what insights and responses did you notice in the classroom? _____

_____

Decontaminating the Classroom

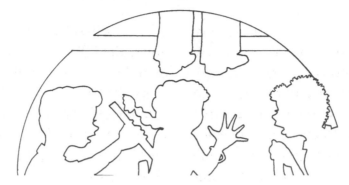

If we are trying to get underway and the class is unruly,

we want to go to our "group discipline" spot.

Locations have memories attached to them. We have all experienced sitting in our living rooms and deciding to do "x." We stood up and were walking to do "x" but were distracted by something. By the time we mentally returned to the original focus, we were baffled because we couldn't remember what our original purpose was. Sheepishly, we returned to the living room couch only to have our memory return just as we sat down.

Once we have their attention, we return to our teaching location as a pleasant teacher.

Decontaminating the Classroom

A teacher is involved in a wide variety of activities in a single day. When the instructor consistently does only one particular activity (e.g., group discipline) from one particular location, the students connect that spot with that activity. Because the educator has established the connection between the activity and that area of the room, the students tend to respond more quickly and more appropriately because they know what to expect. This connection applies not only to location but in all non-verbal communication. For instance, if the teacher consistently turns the overhead on when he wants the class to take notes, the pupils are signaled by the sound of the click of the switch, the noise of the fan and the brightness from the screen area.

Group Discipline

By knowing what activities you do in a week, you can select which activities you want to connect with a given location, face, voice, body posture and perhaps a prop. These will range from taking roll, abstract processing, class discussions, listening circle to one-on-one counseling and group discipline. Therefore, the concept of decontaminating fits in all four phases of a lesson. It is placed here because the single most important activity to have a definite location for is "group discipline," which is definitely a way of getting the class' attention.

You will select three or four activities that you really want to be systematic about. Please include "group discipline" because this activity depletes a teacher's energy faster than any other. Effective group discipline is when we act in a way that is effective for shifting the class into the appropriate learning mode. To do this we need to control our own feelings. This ability to be dissociated is assisted by having a certain location in the room that you go to only if you are going to do "group discipline."

Dissociated

In the book, Righting the Educational Conveyor Belt (by Michael Grinder, Metamorphous Press, 1989) the concept of being dissociated when you discipline is more fully explained. Suffice it to say that "we are never paid to feel when we discipline." This allows us to act in a fashion that is appropriate for where the class is. We can therefore select a style of reprimand that fits what they need at the time.

Your name _____

Decontaminating the Classroom

1. List three or four activities that you really want to be systematic about. "Group Discipline" has already been listed: _Group Discipline,_ _____ ,

_____ & _____ .

2. Relist each of these activities separately and describe where you will do each and what your voice, face and body posture will be for each.

A. Activity: Group Discipline

Location: _____

Voice: _____

Face: _____

Body: _____

B. Activity: _____

Location: _____

Voice: _____

Face: _____

Body: _____

C. Activity: _____

Location: _____

Voice: _____

Face: _____

Body: _____

Do the above systematic use of non-verbal cues for at least two weeks so that you and the class are past the novelty time period.* The best time to initiate a new process like the above is at a natural break in the school year (e.g., spring break). Reflect on the differences between this new system compared to what you formerly did.

* Because of the complexities of the use of location, voice, face and body posture when working with groups, a separate book is devoted to group dynamics: *A Healthy Classroom*.

Mouse Doodles

Be ambitious enough to be patient.
Practice one skill a week.

The self-winding wrist watch was realized in 1939—16 years after it was first conceived. Cellophane was first conceived in 1900. How long before it was realized?

Break & Breathe

**Least Recommended
HIGH BREATHING**

**Recommended
LOW BREATHING**

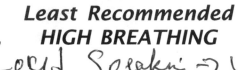

Loud Speaking → use a deep low breath after

Medical Research

Medical research shows the correlation between breathing and the release of chemicals in the body.

- When we breathe high (e.g., as when we raise our voices), we release chemicals of "fight or flight."

- Hearing the raised voice also causes the listeners, both those who are behaving appropriately and those who are not, to release chemicals of stress.

- When we have to say something loudly and if we follow it with a deep abdominal breath, we produce chemicals of calmness.

- During our pause, the listeners will take their cues from us and also breathe lower.

When we find ourselves having breathed high, we can breathe even lower if we move our bodies as we take the deep breath.

Your name _____

Break & Breathe

Every mental state is both represented and maintained by an equivalent physical state. The relationship between the mind-body is so interconnected that a change in one state will be reflected in the other.

If the mental state one is in is not desired or appropriate, then shifting the body assists the change in the mental state. To greatly assist the shift in the emotional and mental state, simultaneously move the body (*Break*) while *Breathing*. This allows a greater separation from the previous state. Of course, the sooner the person recognizes the inappropriateness of the current state, the easier it is to break the state. This is why doing *Break & Breathe* at the end of group discipline (see *Decontaminating the Classroom*) allows the teacher and pupils to return to content and have amnesia regarding the group discipline that occurred. The other occasion that *Break & Breathe* is used is when we need to raise our voice to get the class' attention (see *ABOVE (Pause) Whisper*). In both the group

discipline and using a loud voice to get their attention, the *Break & Breathe* maneuver separates our persona of a martinet from our persona as a kind, loving teacher.

Because the *Break & Breathe* is ENVoY's single most important stress management technique, we recommend that you wait to fill out this form on the following occasions:

- Group Discipline (*Decontaminating the Classroom*)

- Individual discipline

- A loud *ABOVE (Pause) Whisper*

- A severe *Incomplete Sentence* on a right-brain day

- An emergency situation where you need to shout

Group Discipline

1. Describe a situation where it was appropriate to do group discipline: _____

_____

2. Describe how you did *Break & Breathe*: _____

_____

3. Describe the beneficial results both for you and the other(s) involved: _____

_____

_____

Your name _____

Break & Breathe

Individual Discipline

Sometimes a teacher is working with student X and has to put student Y, who is across the room, back on task. We know it is better to use a minimal verbal message both for Y's self-esteem and so as not to disturb the other students who are on task (see *Maintaining the Productive Atmosphere: Mini MITS*). On this occasion, the teacher needs to raise his voice and verbally reprimand Y. If, when the teacher refocuses his attention back to X, he still has residue left from having corrected Y, then X may unduly receive emotional debris. Therefore, when finishing with Y, the teacher wants to stand straight up (and do a half step to the side) and breathe fully. The bigger the state that one wants to get out of, the more important it is to breathe deeply twice.

1. Describe a situation where you did individual discipline: _____

    _____

2. Describe how you did *Break & Breathe*: _____

    _____

3. Describe the beneficial results both for you and the other(s) involved: _____

    _____

    _____

A Loud ABOVE (Pause) Whisper

Sometimes the collective volume is loud and therefore we have to do a loud, "Class!" *(ABOVE)*. The difficulty is that we are susceptible to getting frustrated as we strain our vocal chords.

1. Describe a situation where you did a loud "Class!" *(ABOVE)* in order to get their attention. _____

    _____

2. Describe how you did *Break & Breathe*: _____

    _____

3. Describe the beneficial results both for you and the other(s) involved: _____

    _____

    _____

Your name _____

Break & Breathe

Severe Incomplete Sentence

As in the previous examples such as a loud *ABOVE (Pause)* Whisper, there are times when the gentle approach to getting their attention isn't sufficient. Sometimes we have to do a sharp *Incomplete Sentence* with a harsh expression on our face. We are usually holding our breath high and shallow in our chest cavity. We want to change before stress sets in.

1. Describe a situation when you did a severe *Incomplete Sentence*. _____

   _____

   _____

2. Describe how you did *Break & Breathe*: _____

   _____

3. Describe the beneficial results both for you and the other(s) involved: _____

   _____

   _____

   _____

Emergency Shout

There are occasions when we need to scream or talk loudly because of an emergency situation. For example, a box of books is about to fall on some students and we scream loudly, "Watch out!" We need to have both ourselves and our students recover from the adrenaline that was released inside our bodies.

1. Describe an emergency situation when you raised your voice: _____

   _____

   _____

2. Describe how you did *Break & Breathe*: _____

   _____

3. Describe the beneficial results both for you and the other(s) involved: _____

   _____

   _____

   _____

Yellow Light

Cooperative Learning

Modern teaching methodology is much more interactive than the approach used in the late '70s. The more times we ask students to switch their focuses from small group work and desk work back to the teacher, the more time it takes us to get them focused. Cooperative Learning is a **curriculum** boon. However, because interactive learning requires three to five times more switching of focuses, we have to be more precise in our **management** skills.

Your name _____

Yellow Light

There are a variety of situations when we need to get the class' attention. Sometimes it is the initial contact, like at the start of the class. Then there are times during the presentation we have the class doing a structured activity. It is respectful to signal them that the time is approaching to direct their attention back to the teacher. By doing the signaling before the actual time for direct instruction, the students can ready themselves. This is especially true when they are working in small groups. Think about what it would be like if we only had red and green lights at intersections; hence, this early warning signal will be labeled *Yellow Light*.

Least Recommended

During a presentation when the students are working independently of the teacher, abruptly switch back to direct instruction.

1. What was the lesson on? _____

_____

2. What was the independent work? _____

_____

3. How did you abruptly announce the focus back to the teacher? _____

_____

During the same lesson, do a *Yellow Light* announcement such as "Two minutes" or "One minute to go." Pay attention to your volume; we want them to be aware of the *Yellow Light* without distracting them from the focus of the activity they're engaged in. Notice if it is helpful to repeat the announcement especially emphasizing the last words in a slow, low, draggy voice.

Recommended

4. What did you say? _____

_____

5. Describe your volume and slowness of voice: _____

_____

6. Describe the difference between 1-3 vs. 4 and 5: _____

_____

_____

Your name _____

Yellow Light

The other occasion to use the *Yellow Light* technique is during your presentation when you want to switch from the interaction of "students and teacher" back to "teacher alone." A typical announcement is, "OK, I will call on Janet and Frank and then we will..." Often, we want to make the announcement in a voice that is different from the voice we use during presentations. You might even say we are using our voice like the commas in a sentence; our voice is parenthetical to the rest of the sentence.

7. What did you say? _____

_____

_____

8. Describe your voice volume: _____

_____

_____

9. How did doing 7 and 8 make the transition from the interactive activity back to a focus on the teacher smoother for the class? _____

_____

_____

_____

_____

Mouse Doodle

Be ambitious enough to be patient.
Practice one skill a week.

Cellophane was realized in 1912—12 years after it was first conceived. Nuclear energy was first conceived in 1919. How long before it was actually realized?

CHAPTER THREE

eaching

GETTING THE CLASS READY — — — — ACTUAL TEACHING TIME

PREP PREP PREP PREP PREP PREP

Chapter Three: Teaching

"Teaching is the art of the elusively obvious."

Watching a master teacher during the Teaching phase of a lesson is like witnessing a Philharmonic conductor—so much is based on all the former rehearsals so that the best is drawn from the students. Often from the back of the room, student teachers know they are seeing brilliance; they just can't recognize what is making the difference. That is because the skilled professional is doing preventive management. Class time is spent with emphasis on learning instead of management. The goal of *ENVoY* is to bring these skills to the explicit level.

Teaching is such a group-oriented phase of the lesson that time given to managing the inappropriate individual has to balance with time taken away from the class as a whole. The following skills are designed to be used for the group as a whole:

Group Skills
- *Raise Your Hand vs. Speak Out Refinements*
- *Overlap*
- *Opposite Side of the Room*
- *Use Action Words Last*

The following skills are especially designed to assist the individual:

One-on-One Skills
- *Increasing Non-verbal Signals*
- *Verbal Rapport With the Hard to Reach*

There is a training that gives the participant feedback on how the teacher does non-verbal acknowledgment and recognition of students. The approach is known as TESA, which stands for Teacher Expectations and Student Achievement. The instructors who are schooled in this learn how unintentionally they favor certain students.

Group Dynamic

If you are tertiary level, deal with adolescents or are involved in adult education, the skills you are looking for are most likely found under Getting Their Attention and Teaching. The gregarious nature of these populations forces the instructor to understand and utilize group dynamic concepts. Because of the complexities of such a subject, an entire book is devoted to group dynamics in a learning environment: *A Healthy Classroom*.

Gender Reminder

When applicable, the teacher is referred to with the female pronoun and the student with the male pronoun.

Raise Your Hand vs. Speak Out Refinements

Content First

Format First

Traditionally, teachers have been given the axiom of asking the **content** question before indicating if the class should shout out the answer, *Raise Your Hand*, or if an individual will be called on. *Raise Your Hand Refinements* will examine whether the pupils' interest in the content question might be a better way of determining if it is effective to ask the content question first.

Raise Your Hand vs. Speak Out Refinements

Raise Your Hand vs. Speak Out utilizes the three formats during presentations or lectures: Teacher Only One Talking, Raise Your Hand and Speak Out. This section will detail whether to announce "Raise Your Hand" or "Speak Out" before or after the content question is asked.

Content First

In traditional classes of teacher methodology, it is recommended that the teacher ask the content question first and then call on a student afterward (process second). This approach certainly does keep all students alert because they never know when they are going to be called upon. This is the norm that is best used, and is quite effective, particularly when the teacher has good classroom management. In essence, we are asking the content before announcing what the format will be "Raise Your Hand" or "Everyone speak out the answer" or the instructor will call on an individual student to say the answer.

Format First

Sometimes asking the content question before the format causes a minor cacophony of reverberating answers. It also doesn't allow us to check the quieter and more reserved students' understanding of the content. Therefore, in this example, it would have been better to have announced the format (e.g., Raise Your Hand or perhaps call on an individual student) before the content question was asked. So how do we know what to say first, the content question or the format? If we always do the same sequence, such as saying the format first, what will happen? Sometimes it works and sometimes it doesn't! For example, if the class is very excited and we say, "Joey, what is the answer to number three?" The format is announced before the class knows what the question is. The result is that the class' energy is appropriately eased. However, if the class were lethargic and we say, "Joey, what is the answer to number three?" we have inadvertently added to the room's apathy. We need the following flexible formula:

Flexible Formula

- If interest in the content is high, then announce the format before asking the content question.

- If interest in the content is low, we have the luxury of announcing the format after stating the content question.

Formats can be sequenced. For example, the teacher could do a Raise Your Hand and, once the majority of the pupils have their hands up, the instructor could switch to having the class Speak Out the answer in unison or turn to a neighbor and say the answer.

Your name _____

Raise Your Hand vs. Speak Out Refinements

Recommended

High Interest Content

Record the results of following the formula in three situations where the interest in the content was high and you announced the format before asking the content question.

1. **First situation**: Date:_____ Time:_____

   How did you know interest in the content was going to be high? _____

   _____

   Circle the format announced: Raise Your Hand, Call on one student, Speak Out, Raise Your Hand then Speak Out the answer in unison or _____

   Describe the results: _____

   _____

2. **Second situation**: Date:_____ Time:_____

   How did you know interest in the content was going to be high? _____

   _____

   Circle the format announced: Raise Your Hand, Call on one student, Speak Out, Raise Your Hand then Speak Out the answer in unison or _____

   Describe the results: _____

   _____

   _____

3. **Third situation**: Date:_____ Time:_____

   How did you know interest in the content was going to be high? _____

   _____

   Circle the format announced: Raise Your Hand, Call on one student, Speak Out, Raise Your Hand then Speak Out the answer in unison or _____

   Describe the results: _____

   _____

   _____

Your name _____

Raise Your Hand vs. Speak Out Refinements

Recommended

Low Interest Content

Record the results of following the formula in three situations where the interest in the content was low and you asked the content question first.

1. **First situation**: Date:_____ Time:_____

   How did you know interest in the content was going to be low? _____

   _____

   After you said the content question, how long did you wait before you announced the format? _____

   Circle the format announced: Raise Your Hand, Call on one student, Speak Out, Raise Your Hand then Speak Out the answer in unison or _____

   Describe the results: _____

2. **Second situation**: Date:_____ Time:_____

   How did you know interest in the content was going to be low? _____

   _____

   After you said the content question, how long did you wait before you announced the format? _____

   Circle the format announced: Raise Your Hand, Call on one student, Speak Out, Raise Your Hand then Speak Out the answer in unison or _____

   Describe the results: _____

3. **Third situation**: Date:_____ Time:_____

   How did you know interest in the content was going to be low? _____

   After you said the content question, how long did you wait before you announced the format? _____

   Circle the format announced: Raise Your Hand, Call on one student, Speak Out, Raise Your Hand then Speak Out the answer in unison or _____

   Describe the results: _____

   _____

Your name _____

Raise Your Hand vs. Speak Out Refinements

Testing the Formula

For a week, you have done the formula of

- interest high = format first,

- interest low = content question first.

To test the validity of this recommendation, we will do the opposite.

Least Recommended

High Interest Content:

During the next several days, when you estimate the interest in the content question will be high, ask the content question first. Record the results of having done this three times.

1. **First situation**: Date:_____ Time:_____

   How did you know the interest in the content was going to be high? _____
   _____

   Describe what happened: _____
   _____

2. **Second situation**: Date:_____ Time:_____

   How did you know the interest in the content was going to be high? _____
   _____

   Describe what happened: _____
   _____

3. **Third situation**: Date:_____ Time:_____

   How did you know the interest in the content was going to be high? _____
   _____

   Describe what happened: _____
   _____

Your name _____

Raise Your Hand vs. Speak Out Refinements

Least Recommended

Low Interest Content

When you estimate that the interest in the content will be low, announce the format first.

1. **First situation**: Date:_____ Time:_____

   How did you know the interest in the content was going to be low? _____

   _____

   Circle the format that was announced: Raise Your Hand, Call on one student, Speak Out, Raise Your Hand and then Speak out the answer in unison or _____

   Describe what happened: _____

2. **Second situation**: Date:_____ Time:_____

   How did you know the interest in the content was going to low? _____

   _____

   Circle the format that was announced: Raise Your Hand, Call on one student, Speak Out, Raise Your Hand and then Speak out the answer in unison or _____

   Describe what happened: _____

3. **Third situation**: Date:_____ Time:_____

   How did you know the interest in the content was going to be low? _____

   _____

   Circle the format that was announced: Raise Your Hand, Call on one student, Speak Out, Raise Your Hand and then Speak out the answer in unison or _____

   Describe what happened: _____

   What conclusions can you draw from doing the recommended formula of "interest high = format first" and "interest low = content question first" compared to the results of doing the least recommended way? _____

   _____

   _____

   _____

Increasing Non-verbal Signals

Home Improvement

While shopping in a hardware store, Gail sent son, Kelly, over to another aisle to buy some wire nuts for electrical wiring. As he walked away, he hollered back, "What size?"

Mom replied, "Get a dozen yellow caps!"

Later in the car he inquired, "How did you know that *yellow* was the right size?"

"Son, you don't always need to know the actual size — just notice the color of the old ones. From a ring on the fourth finger of the left hand to three different colored lights at intersections, the world is made up of the non-verbals of colors, sizes, shapes..."

In *Increasing Non-verbal Signals* an example of a teacher using the auditory non-verbal signal of tapping on the board will be used.

The systematic use of **visual, auditory**, and **kinesthetic** non-verbal signals is the basis of brilliant classroom communication.

Increasing Non-verbal Signals

One of the biggest benefits for being systematic with non-verbal signals is that the teacher is able to cover more content in more of a "win-win" atmosphere. How? By using non-verbal signals for management, your voice can be used for the "pace of the lesson." For example, the teacher slowly turns off the lights and then turns them back on. The class looks up because they know that turning off and on the lights means the teacher needs the pupils' attention.

Academic Non-verbals

As teachers, we agree that non-verbal signals for management are both desirable and effective, but *ENVoY* suggests that non-verbal signals for academic purposes are also most welcome and efficient. Our contention is that when non-verbal signals are used during our academic presentation (e.g., a hand gesture to indicate we are referring to the top number in a fraction), these non-verbal messages are preventive management techniques. How? Because they force the class to watch the instructor. This results in a quieter room and with the students looking at the teacher, non-verbal signals from the instructor are more available to use. For example, if the teacher has written on the board

$$\begin{array}{r} 27 \\ \times\ 13 \\ \hline \end{array}$$

and says, "Class, what is 13 x 27?" the instructor is being totally auditory; a student could follow the lesson without looking at the teacher. However, if the teacher were less specific, "Class, what is 13 x this number?" as she points to the "27," the class has to visually pay attention to the teacher at the board.

WIN-WIN

Your name _____

Increasing Non-verbal Signals

Systematic Non-verbal Signals

Fill this out on one of your lessons. Of course, it is easier to remember the non-verbal signals if you fill out this sheet immediately following the lesson.

In the left column list all academic and management (especially the latter) non-verbal signals done during 10 minutes of the Teaching portion of the lesson. To the right, describe the usage and meaning of the non-verbal signals.

Non-verbal Signals		Usage/Meaning

a. _____ = _____

_____ = _____

b _____ = _____

_____ = _____

c. _____ = _____

_____ = _____

d. _____ = _____

_____ = _____

e. _____ = _____

_____ = _____

f. _____ = _____

_____ = _____

g. _____ = _____

_____ = _____

Your name _____

Increasing Non-verbal Signals

Our goal is to literally use our non-verbal signals for the format and our verbal level for the content. List those occasions when you used a verbal signal when it might have been more effective to either use a non-verbal signal with it or even just use the non-verbal signal alone. For instance, the instructor notices that when she turns the overhead on, the students pick up their pens to take notes on visually shown information. But, after the students have copied the information, they gradually put their pens down or play with them. Reflecting on this observation, the teacher concludes that once the students have finished copying the information, it would be more effective to turn off the overhead. This will keep the connection of "overhead on" equals "be attentive."

Becoming Systematic

Non-verbal Signals		Usage/Meaning
a. _____	=	_____
	=	_____
b _____	=	_____
	=	_____
c. _____	=	_____
	=	_____
d. _____	=	_____
	=	_____

Mention the insights you have gathered from this activity.

_____

_____

_____

_____

_____

Overlap

Research doesn't paint a very pretty picture

Transition

Research doesn't paint a very pretty picture of how efficiently we are able to make transitions. Sometimes it seems the teaching locomotive spends more time getting the passengers ready to travel than actually taking them to where they need to go. During transition we have to increase the precision of management skills so we can get back to why we chose our profession—to teach knowledge, impart skills, and facilitate self-esteem.

Overlap

Throughout any forty-five minute period, the teacher will have times in which she needs the class' attention and other times when the students are working independently from the teacher. Later, the teacher may need the class' attention again. Basically, what we have is activity A, then a transition to activity B, then a transition to activity C. The number of activities determines the number of times Getting Their Attention is required. So what is the disadvantage of this traditional way of doing transition?

Saving Time

When the students are finishing activity A, there is a shuffle in the room (e.g., the students put their books away). Then the teacher does a Getting Their Attention and announces activity B. To save time, the teacher uses the Overlap technique by announcing activity B before activity A is finished. For example, the teacher is orchestrating the class' recitation of the answers to the five questions at the end of the chapter. Then they will be putting their books away and taking out another book and beginning activity B. The *Overlap* technique is that as we finish the answer to question number four, the teacher announces, "Before we do number five, take out..." She announces and shows directions on how to do activity B on the board. The students take out materials for activity B. Then number 5 is read and orally answered. We are automatically into activity B without any down time.

Kinesthetic Class

Of course, it is important to consider the concentration capacity of the class and whether the pause/break between activity A and activity B is helpful. For example, the greater the percentage of kinesthetic students in the classroom, the greater the necessity to allow movement in order to help them actually comply with sitting still.

Your name _____

Overlap

During the next three days, at least once a day, do the *Overlap* transition technique and briefly describe what was involved. Mention if some or all of the directions are visually displayed and if there are some directions that are used often enough to warrant lamination.

1. Date: _____

   _____

   _____

   _____

2. Date: _____

   _____

   _____

   _____

3. Date: _____

   _____

   _____

   _____

4. Summarize the overall insights and responses that were elicited from using this activity.

   _____

   _____

   _____

   _____

   _____

   _____

   _____

   _____

   _____

Mouse Doodles

Be ambitious enough to be patient.
Practice one skill a week.

Nuclear energy was finally realized in 1965—46 years after it was conceived. Liquid shampoo was first considered in 1950. How long do you think it took to realize?

Opposite Side of the Room

Pyrrhic Victory

In the late '60s, I was privileged to be personally trained by Carl Rogers. He understood, and to some extent, defined rapport. His name is synonymous with the non-verbal communication of empathy when we are listening:

- leaning towards the person,

- nodding our heads,

- and making sounds when the person says his important points.

These skills usually result in a warm, cooperative atmosphere.

Most of us are so trained in these one-on-one techniques that sometimes we have the Pyrrhic Victory of gaining rapport with one student while losing the group rapport. We need to create techniques that foster group rapport while maintaining the one-on-one closeness. *Opposite Side of the Room* is such a technique.

Your name _____

Opposite Side of the Room

The ideal in presenting or lecturing is to have our content and, more importantly, our delivery be so intriguing that our students are absorbed. This is the ultimate in preventive management. But, alas, some of us don't live in an "educational Camelot." A practical rule of thumb is to use the verbal level for the imparting of content and use our nonverbal skills for management. We know that the kinesthetic learner is affected by the physical presence of the teacher. Therefore, moving around the room while presenting, especially being in the neighborhood of the kinesthetic learners, is preventive management. This group dynamic technique would be easy to accomplish except for a habit that we have learned from one-on-one rapport, which is to move toward the questioner or the person we call on.

When you are in the front of the room, move toward the student you call upon. Or if a student asks a question, move in the direction of that student. This is the traditional style of rapport.

Your natural tendency is to move toward the student you call on. However, you can manage the entire class more effectively by verbally engaging the student from a distance. Without looking at the student you plan to call on, intentionally walk to the side of the room away from this student. Once you are away from the student you are planning to call upon, turn back toward him and look at this student and call on him. You now have your eyes on the student who is far from you and your body is close to other students. Your voice and body tend to keep the students who are physically close to you attentive while your gaze keeps the students farther away also appropriate.

Least Recommended

For two days, do the traditional style of rapport. When you are in the front of the room, move toward the student you call upon. Or, if a student asks a question, move in the direction of that student. Describe your observations here: _____

_____

_____

Recommended

For two days, do this "Opposite Side of the Room" management technique. Report the difference in attentiveness from the students when you are using this maneuver as compared to the traditional style of rapport: _____

_____

_____

Verbal Rapport With Hard To Reach Students

Being the owners of both dogs and cats, Gail and I are convinced that God provides us with the former to make us feel successful as non-verbal communicators and gives us the latter to keep us humble.

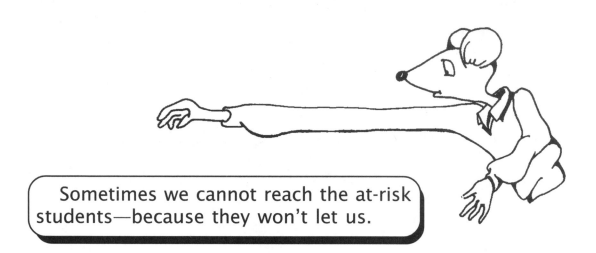

Sometimes we cannot reach the at-risk students—because they won't let us.

We have to leave a trail that intrigues and spices their interest—so they will reach towards us.

What's your formula for cinnamon sugar?

Your name _____

Verbal Rapport With Hard To Reach Students

There is a certain percentage of students who are not motivated by the teacher's credentials or authority. While each school varies, five to fifteen percent of the school's population are hard to reach. Inner city schools will experience the highest percentage. Overall, this population is rapidly increasing. The hard to reach are usually right-brain students who are more or less not affected by standard discipline systems. These students can be reached through some form of rapport. One form of rapport is to include in our lesson something that is of high interest to them. They then become much more attentive.

First Student

1. First student's initials: _____

2. Briefly describe the student's behaviors that indicate he is *Hard to Reach*.

   _____

   _____

   _____

   _____

3. When acting in a capacity other than the authoritarian position of teacher (during transition, at school events, passing in the halls), interact with the student. Find the student's two or three highest positive topics of interest. List them here:

   • _____

   • _____

   • _____

4. When presenting or lecturing or working one-on-one, spice the conversation with items from the student's high-interest areas to hold his attention. List two examples of how you did this:

   • _____

   • _____

5. Describe the increase in the student's attentiveness. _____

   _____

   _____

   _____

Your name _____

Verbal Rapport with Hard to Reach Students

Second Student

1. Second student's initials: _____

2. Briefly describe the student's behaviors that indicate he is *Hard to Reach*. _____

_____

_____

_____

_____

_____

3. When acting in a capacity other than the authoritarian position of teacher (during transition, at school events, passing in the halls), interact with the student. Find the student's two or three highest positive topics of interest. List them here:

   • _____

   • _____

   • _____

4. When presenting or lecturing or working one-on-one, spice the conversation with items from the student's high-interest areas to hold his attention. List two examples of how you did this:

   • _____

   _____

   • _____

   _____

5. Describe the increase in the student's attentiveness. _____

_____

_____

_____

Verbal Rapport with Hard to Reach Students

Adolescents and Above

When teaching in the lower grades, the teacher can look at the student as the instructor talks about that particular student's area of high interest. When teaching adolescents and adults, it is more effective not to look at the student as the instructor sprinkles bits of that student's high-interest area into the discussion. Why? One trait that separates the right-brain oriented student from the rest of the school population is his tendency to be "self-selective." He reserves the right to choose relationships with others, especially people in positions of authority. This student doesn't want others deciding to form relationships with him; therefore, if the teacher looks at the pupil when saying the high-interest item, the student knows the teacher is intentionally using the ploy. Their range of reactions include: "Leave me alone," "I don't want to be manipulated by you," "Boy, are you easy for me to control," "This classroor just became mine."

Intrigue

As we begin to say their area of high interest and notice that they are starting to look toward us, we want to partially turn away from them. By not looking directly at them, they don't know if we brought up the subject because of them or if we are interested in that subject ourselves. They become drawn to us. That intrigues them and these students love being intrigued. Behaviorally, their eyes are following us as we turn away from them. They are chasing, choosing, selecting us.

Your name _____

Verbal Rapport with Hard to Reach Students

Adolescent and Above

1. **First person's** initials or description who is right-brain oriented: _____

2. List the person's two or three high-interest items: _____
_____
_____

3. While you are lecturing and the targeted student isn't attentive, include one of that student's high-interest areas in the discussion. As you notice him beginning to look your way, partially turn away. Describe what you said and did: _____
_____
_____
_____

4. Describe the change in the student's attentiveness. _____
_____
_____

1. **Second person's** initials or description who is right-brain oriented: _____

2. List the person's two or three high-interest items: _____
_____
_____

3. While you are lecturing and the targeted student isn't attentive, include one of that student's high-interest areas in the discussion. As you notice him beginning to look your way, partially turn away. Describe what you said and did: _____
_____
_____

4. Describe the change in the student's attentiveness. _____
_____
_____

Your name _____

Verbal Rapport with Hard to Reach Students
Timing

The longer a person is inattentive, the stronger his daydream becomes. The longer one is in the same physical state, the deeper into the mental state the person goes. Every mental state is represented and maintained by the physical posture. Therefore, as soon as we see the student start to fade from attentiveness and we mention his high-interest item, the more likely he is to hear our comment.

Let's test this contention by doing the opposite of the axiom and then doing the axiom. If you are unable to do number 3-6 during the lesson, then do 3 and 5 during the same lesson and 4 and 6 during another lesson. Once you have completed the following activity, reflect on what insights you have gained by comparing the results obtained by 3 and 4 with using the recommended method of 5 and 6. Later on in Chapter Five, the skill *Power to Influence* will mention the concept "Vacuum Pause." Once you have learned this concept, you will be even more effective when you mention the student's high-interest item during his vacuum pause.

---

1. Initials or description of a right-brain oriented student: _____

2. List the person's high-interest items: _____

Least Recommended

3. While you are lecturing and you notice the student is fading from attentiveness, just continue your presentation. Let the student go completely into his selected state. Once you know he is solidly concentrating on something other than your lecture, spice your content with the student's high interest item. Describe your voice volume and any changes in the student's attentiveness: _____

4. Do this same maneuver again with the same student. It would be best to do a repeat of this same technique during the same lecture. Describe your voice volume and any changes in the student's attentiveness. _____

Recommended

5. Now sprinkle the high-interest area into your presentation just as he starts to fade from attentiveness. Try to do this during the same lesson as 3. As much as possible, keep your voice volume at the same level as it was in 3. This will allow for a more accurate comparison between the two. Describe your voice volume and the degree that the student becomes attentive. _____

6. Do this recommended way again. Try to do this during the same lesson as 4. As much as possible, keep your voice volume at the same level as it was in 4. Reflect on the connection between your voice volume and the degree that the student becomes attentive.

Use Action Words Last

In the military, there is an expression, "Follow the last order first." However, in school when students hear any action words like, "Take...," "Open to...," "We will now do...," "Make room for...," the students:

· activate their bodies

· decrease their ability to hear.

We want to use Action Words Last!

Use Action Words Last

When students hear a teacher say action words such as "take," "open," "do," "make," etc., their bodies are activated. When the students' bodies are activated, their hearing decreases as the body increases in movement. When a teacher says, "Take out your book and turn to page number forty-three," hearing the words, "Take out..." will activate the students to be in their desks pulling out their books. Some of them won't be able to hear the page number so that the teacher ends up repeating it. The instructor has inadvertently caused a segmenting of the classroom. There is the instructor, those students who have their books open to page forty-three and those students who are lost. In essence, the lesson is slightly out-of-sync. There are a couple of ways of getting around this:

- Whenever possible, say the action words last. For instance, "On page 43, you will find in the science book you're now taking out..."

- If you need to say an action word, the safer way to say an action word is to freeze the students while you talk. Use a non-verbal gesture such as your hand forward in a traffic cop style position of "stop" as you say, "In just a minute you're going to be taking out your science book and looking at page 43." Make sure you hold the non-verbal gesture until you want them to do it.

- Of course, the safest way to communicate instructions is to visually display the specifics on the board or overhead "pg. 43" as we say, "On page 43..." The visual approach is what we want to do on right-brain days.

USE ACTION WORDS LAST

Your name _____

Use Action Words Last

Least Recommended

For the next two days, design lessons that include action words. Test the above axiom by doing the reverse of the recommended approach. This way you can compare the difference between the traditional placement of action words at the beginning of the instructions versus the suggested approach of either the action words later or the use of non-verbal gestures to freeze the class or both.

1. List the actions words you said: _____

   _____

2. Intentionally place your action words at the beginning of the instructions. List the instructions that followed the action words: _____

   _____

3. Describe what percentage of the class responded appropriately. Note which specific students didn't respond appropriately. _____

   _____

4. Comment on how out-of-sync this segment of the lesson was: _____

   _____

Recommended

Now switch to the recommended approach. Either say the action words at the end of the instructions and/or use a non-verbal gesture to hold the pupils still as you say the instructions.

1. List the action words said: _____

2. Apart from the action words, what were the instructions given? _____

   _____

3. Describe your placement of the action words. If a non-verbal gesture was used, what was the gesture, and did you hold this signal until you finished the instructions? _____

   _____

4. Describe what percentage of the class responded appropriately. Note which specific students didn't respond appropriately. _____

   _____

5. Reflect on if this segment of the lesson seemed more in sync using the recommended approach.

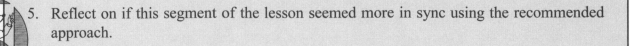

Your name _____

Use Action Words Last

Do the recommended approach again.

1. List the action words said: _____

   _____

2. Apart from the action words, what were the instructions given? _____

   _____

   _____

3. Describe your placement of the action words. If a non-verbal gesture was used, what was the gesture, and did you hold this signal until you finished the instructions? _____

   _____

4. Describe what percentage of the class responded appropriately. Note which specific students didn't respond appropriately. _____

   _____

5. Comment on if using the recommended approach seems to make the lesson and group dynamics more in sync. _____

   _____

What have you noticed in the difference in the students' responsiveness between the approach used in number 1 compared to the recommended approach of number 2. If it was a right-brain day, did you use the board or overhead to show the specifics of the instructions? If yes, how were the students affected by you using action words last?

CHAPTER FOUR

Transition to Seatwork

Literature
Read p. 87-96
Answer in full the
10 questions on p. 97

Chapter Four: Transition to Seatwork

"If a man does not know to which port he is sailing,
no wind is favorable."

Seneca

The next chapter is Seatwork. Trying to be efficient during this segment of the lesson is the bane of all teachers. We are constantly managing the group in the hopes that we can assist individuals one-on-one. In business there is an expression that managers spend eighty percent of their time with twenty percent of the people they supervise. Translated into an educational setting, during seatwork we spend sixty to eighty percent of our time with the same four to six students.

Productivity

Why mention seatwork concerns here? The productivity of seatwork is a by-product of how we set sail as we leave the harbor of teaching and navigate into seatwork. The skills of this chapter are the fewest in the book. But don't be fooled by length. For non-verbal techniques to be used during seatwork, there have to be clear and concise visual directions given during the transition into seatwork. These directions need to be visual during the entirety of the Seatwork phase of the lesson for the verbal management to be kept to the minimum. Therefore, make sure your motivation for a good seatwork atmosphere is transferred to mastering these Transition skills: *Exit Directions* and *Most Important Twenty Seconds.*

Relationships

Since one of the main purposes of *ENVoY* is to switch our profession from one of Power Management to Management by Influence, any and all directions that can be visually represented help preserve the relationship between the teacher and the students who need management. How? When a teacher orally reminds a student of what she should be doing, the student unconsciously associates the teacher with the resultant feelings of having been reprimanded. When the teacher gets the student's attention and non-verbally directs her to look and follow the board's directions—this is the location of the command, instead of the teacher. In the former scenario, there are only two parties present: the teacher and the student; technically this is called "negotiation." In the latter scene, there are figuratively three parties present: the board, the student and the teacher; hence, the term "mediation." The teacher can be seen by the student as facilitating. If the teacher is seen as the "bad guy" at least the board shares some of the blame. Therefore, whenever possible, have a visual representation of the directive.

Chapter Four: Transition to Seatwork

Commonalities

Because of the innate overlap between the skills of the Transition to Seatwork skills and the actual skills once in the Seatwork phase of the lesson, there are four skillsheets that could have been rightfully placed in either chapter. Their titles indicate their commonalities:

Advanced Exit Directions

Maintaining the Productive Atmosphere: Mini MITS

Maintaining the Productive Atmosphere: Private Voice

Maintaining the Productive Atmosphere: Walking Speed

These are listed here in their order of importance but not presented in this sequence in the chapter. The skillsheet *Advanced Exit Directions* is ideal through grade five and is effective if modified for grades above that.

Gender Reminder

When applicable, the teacher is referred to with the male pronoun and the student with the female pronoun.

Mouse Doodles

Be ambitious enough to be patient.
Practice one skill a week.

Liquid Shampoo was realized in 1958—eight years after it was first conceived. The automatic transmission was first conceived in 1930. How long before it was finally realized?

Exit Direction Refinements

If Gary Larson, the creator of the *Far Side*, ever did an educational comedy movie, he might include the following scene from a very left-brain school. Instead of posting a diagram by the door of how to proceed during a fire drill, the information is written out in sentences. The substitute is conscientiously holding up the class from exiting while she finishes reading the exact route the class is supposed to take. As some students moan and groan, she says over her shoulder, "Well, if you are getting too warm, move away from the flames—I am almost done reading!"

Usually it is not a question of whether the students can read the *Exit Directions* or not. The real question is "Will they...?" Because the at-risk student thinks in objects instead of words, use graphics. One smart teacher took the textbook to a local print shop and made an enlarged color copy that could be easily seen from the back of the room. He placed a white square in the middle of the cover. Once finished, he laminated this poster. In the white square, the teacher used a washable overhead transparency pen to write the page and problems/questions assigned for the day.

Your name _____

Exit Direction Refinements

In *Exit Directions* (pp 30-31), the suggestions were:

- Visual directions provide greater clarity and double the length of memory.

- Consistently and systematically use a certain location and colors for exit directions.

- Laminate the information that is used on a regular basis.

There are some additional suggestions that may further assist you in this transition from the Teaching portion of your lesson to the Seatwork/homework segment. Because of the nature of these skills, you may want to invite an observer to come in after you have implemented one technique before you learn the next one.

Silently Point

It would be unrealistic for us to think that students can switch overnight from the previous format of asking us to repeat the *Exit Directions* during seatwork to actually reading them from the board. During Seatwork, when the pupils ask questions that are answered on the board (e.g., "What do I do next?"), learn to point to the board in silence. It is very important that you do this without having eye contact with the student who is asking. You want to avoid eye contact so that the student does not perceive this as a way of getting attention from you. Describe how long it took most students to get used to reading the board during Seatwork, who took longer to form the habit and how you silently pointed to the board:

_____

Queries

When you announce the *Exit Directions* and show them on the board or laminated cards, ask, "Any questions?" When you are responding to their queries, in addition to orally answering, make sure you write the information on the board; otherwise, you will probably give the same oral information several more times.

Experiment with this contention by doing the reverse: for the next two days announce the *Exit Directions* and write them on the board or cards. Ask, "Any questions?" Answer all queries orally and describe how many times you have to repeat the same information:

_____

_____

Then for two days, besides orally answering the questions, write the answers to any queries you are asked on the board and describe if the extra effort of writing is worth the results you get: _____

Exit Direction Refinements

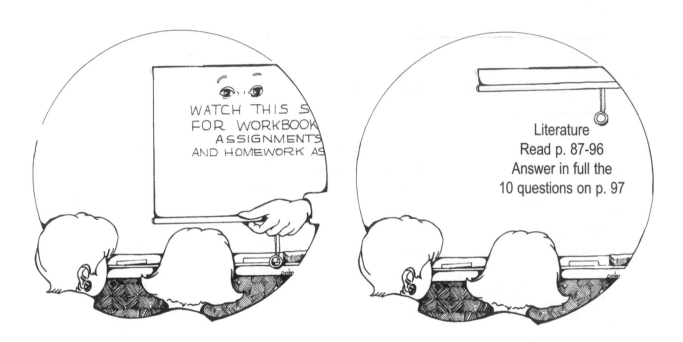

Hidden and Then Exposed

There are advantages in keeping the directions hidden until you have finished the **Teaching** portion of the lesson and it is time to release the class to start the **Seatwork**/homework.

Your name _____

Exit Direction Refinements

Graphics

The right-brain students tend to pay more attention to graphics, symbols and real objects instead of words. Include these in both your laminated cards and when you write on the board as much as possible. For example, if the teacher were using a workbook, he could color copy the cover and laminate it. Then by using magnets, he could put it on the board and write the page number next to it. This is a very fast and convenient way of doing your *Exit Directions*. Describe your new graphics and what they represent: _____

_____

_____

Describe how certain students are helped by the graphics: _____

_____

_____

Hidden and Then Exposed

In classrooms where the teacher posts the *Exit Directions* before or during the lecture, some students will start them during the teacher's presentation. There are advantages to keeping the directions hidden until you have finished the Teaching portion of the lesson and it is time to release the class to start the seatwork/homework. To write out lengthy *Exit Directions* at the time you are finishing the lecture/presentation is often slow and can create some management problems.

So how can we have prepared *Exit Directions* and the option of exposing them in a timely fashion? This can be done by having the laminated cards placed on the chalk tray with their backs to the class. Or if you have written them, hide them under a map that is pulled down.

Test this contention. For the next two days, start a presentation with the *Exit Directions* exposed. Describe any management difficulties that arise: _____

_____

_____

Then for the next two days, prepare the *Exit Directions* but keep them hidden and then expose them in a timely fashion. Describe if the extra effort of preparing them ahead of time is worth the results you get: _____

_____

_____

Advanced Exit Directions

The mind more quickly recognizes and processes non-verbal symbols (e.g., hand gestures) than words. A signal can convey a tremendous amount of information in a very short amount of time. An example of the difference in the verbal and non-verbal levels of communication is the history of the computer. Originally one navigated around the computer by typing in words. Now, the tool bars on today's machines communicate with god-sent clarity and speed.

When we use signals to put a student ON task, we can do so without looking at the student—thus preserving the relationship.

Advanced Exit Directions

This skill uses concepts from both *Exit Directions* and from *OFF/Neutral/On*. Make sure you have done both before practicing this skill. When the class is on task and the teacher sees someone behaving inappropriately, he wants to shift the student toward being on task as silently as possible. The silence maintains the productive atmosphere. The *Exit Directions* allow the minimal verbal communication. *Advanced Exit Directions* is a process of numbering the directions on the board. This will allow the teacher, during seatwork, to silently refer to particular parts of the *Exit Directions*. For example, the teacher has numbered the following *Exit Directions*:

1. Math = page 57 # 1 - 15, show your work, due at end of class.

2. Spelling = Ch. 9, due this Friday

3. When you finish, you may do free reading.

For instance, through grade five the teacher can teach the class to use two fingers from each hand and make the symbol that we associate with the "X" and "O" game commonly called "cat." ("#"). This is also the symbol for number. When a teacher sees a student OFF task, the teacher can say the student's name and the pupil looks at the instructor who shows non-verbally the # symbol and slowly looks at the board. This clues the student to look at the board and to silently signal back to the teacher which number the student is working on. After the fifth grade, the students most likely will not allow the teacher to use the # symbol. Therefore, we would need to non-verbally signal the equivalent of #. For example we could say the student's name and when the pupil looks at us, we redirect her attention to the board and shrug our shoulders and mouth, "Which one are you on?"

Guarantees

Advanced Exit Directions guarantees that the teacher knows that the student is aware of what her ON task focus is.

This technique avoids the auditory channel, which is especially useful in working with adolescents. Do this three times during the coming week and record your results in terms of the speed at which students get back on task and the rest of the class maintains a productive atmosphere.

Remember to wait until the student has gone ON task and breathed twice before you return to what you were doing.

Your name _____

Advanced Exit Directions

First Example

1. Student's initials who you put ON task: _____

2. Non-verbal signal used by teacher: _____

3. Reaction of student: _____

4. Did you wait until the student went ON task and had breathed at least twice before you resumed what you were doing?   **YES/NO**

5. Were students who were ON task oblivious to the maneuver?   **YES/NO**

6. Reflect on the ON task students' reactions or lack of reactions to your using *Advanced Exit Directions*.

Second Example

1. Student's initials who you put ON task: _____

2. Non-verbal signal used by teacher: _____

3. Reaction of student: _____

4. Did you wait until the student went ON task and had breathed at least twice before you resumed what you were doing?   **YES/NO**

5. Were students who were ON task oblivious to the maneuver?   **YES/NO**

6. Reflect on the ON task students' reactions or lack of reactions to your using *Advanced Exit Directions*.

Third Example

1. Student's initials who you put ON task: _____

2. Non-verbal signal used by teacher: _____

3. Reaction of student: _____

4. Did you wait until the student went ON task and had breathed at least twice before you resumed what you were doing?   **YES/NO**

5. Were students who were ON task oblivious to the maneuver?   **YES/NO**

6. Reflect on the ON task students' reactions or lack of reactions to your using *Advanced Exit Directions*.

Mouse Doodles

Be ambitious enough to be patient.
Practice one skill a week.

The automatic transmission was finally realized in 1946—16 years after it was first conceived. Antibiotics were first conceived in 1910. How long before they were finally realized?

Maintaining the Productive Atmosphere
Private Voice

Least Recommended

Auditory Oriented Teachers

As educators we are famous for having a "teacher's voice." We also can be infamous for such a voice. If we use the teaching voice while helping students individually, the other students learn to tune us out. Teachers who are athletic coaches especially have to watch their tendency to talk in a commanding manner.

During Seatwork, we are moving around the room assisting students one-on-one. This is the time we want a Private Voice. This will allow the students to concentrate.

Recommended

When not Teaching, there is a second reason for using a Private Voice. Like the boy who cried wolf too many times, if we use a Public Voice during the individual work times, the pupils become numb to our loud voice. When it is actually time to get the class' attention, they don't respond as well.

Your name _____

Maintaining the Productive Atmosphere
Private Voice

We know that more productive seatwork occurs because of a visual atmosphere that starts with the teacher doing *Visual Directions* and *MITS*. How is this atmosphere maintained and fostered once the *Most Important Twenty Seconds* is up? This skillsheet will cover one of the three factors that is conducive to the productive motif.

Public vs. Private Voice

Students have been conditioned over their school career to respond to the teacher's call for attention. We know that this request can be both verbally done (e.g., "Class," "Boys and girls," "Gang," "Quiet please," "Look this way," etc.) and non-verbally. One of the primary ways that the pupils are non-verbally signaled to give the instructor attention is the teacher's voice. It is impera-

tive that we pay attention to whether we are using a public or private voice. We want to do the former during presentations and the latter during Seatwork time.

To test this contention, during Seatwork the teacher will do the opposite: use the public lecture voice while assisting a student one-on-one. Notice how students will tend to shift their bodies. Sometimes our public teaching voice will be like a stone in a pond with reverberations of students' movements. The students closer to the teacher shift more than those farther away. At other times, those students close to the teacher will freeze and those farther away may move. Sometimes if our voice is angry and loud, the students freeze like frightened animals who are being stalked.

Public Voice

1. Describe your voice pattern in terms of volume and length of speaking: _____

_____

_____

2. Describe the students' reactions; specifically, how soon after you began the public voice did they begin to shift, when they stopped and if certain sections of the room were more affected than others: _____

_____

Private Voice

3. Immediately follow the above with several one-on-one interactions with students using a private voice and notice, hopefully, the lack of the students shifting their bodies. Reflect if the productive atmosphere is maintained better with the *Private Voice*.

Maintaining the Productive Atmosphere
Walking Speed

Least Recommended   **Recommended**

Kinesthetic Oriented Teachers

Walking Speed is designed for kinesthetic-oriented teachers. While our passion and enthusiasm are our strengths, they can also be our liabilities. Productive Seatwork reminds us of a sports event. After it is over, we want to remember what the players did, not what the ref/umpire did. Likewise, during Seatwork the time is for the student not the teacher. If we move too fast, we are like a boat going by people concentrating on their fishing. We disturb them as they bob in our wake.

Your name _____

Maintaining the Productive Atmosphere
Walking Speed

In *Maintaining the Productive Atmosphere: Private Voice* we explored the effect our voice has on the class' concentration during seatwork. The focus of this skill is on the consequence of the teacher's walking speed as he moves about the room assisting students one- on-one.

When teachers walk too fast around the room, they are like a boat going through water—there is a wake behind them.

Least Recommended

During Seatwork, intentionally move rapidly from one side of the room to the other side. Describe where you moved to and from and the speed: _____

_____

_____

Describe the effect it had on the students. Be specific as to whether those students most affected by it were close or farther away from the path. Especially pay attention to the kinesthetic learners (Attention Deficit Disorder/Hyperactive/etc.): _____

_____

_____

_____

You may want to do the above more than once because the cumulative effect of the wake is geometric. Picture a wake hitting the sides of a closed pond and then bouncing off the side only to clash with the next set of ripples coming in from the repeated passes from a speedboat.

Recommended

Immediately switch to a calm, slow movement pattern and describe the effect and, hopefully, the lack of ripples in the students' ability to concentrate: _____

_____

_____

Summarize the effects of your walking speed on the students' productivity; especially the kinesthetic learners: _____

_____

_____

Maintaining the Productive Atmosphere
Mini MITS

Educational Igors

As teachers we are really hard workers. That is one of the reasons it is so hard to stand still during the *Most Important Twenty Seconds*—we feel best about ourselves when we are working/helping/imparting to others. Our profession is seen as being "in service to others" and "being excellent explainers;" hence, the first civilian selected to go into outer space was a teacher.

If we watched a video of ourselves during **Seatwork**, we would often see that we don't stand up straight as we finish helping one student and going to help another. Comically speaking, we become hunched over like Educational Igors. When we pause and stand up between helping students, we literally help our bodies so we have more energy for the whole day, as well as the effect of the class quieting down.

Your name _____

Maintaining the Productive Atmosphere
Mini MITS

From *Exit Directions* and *Most Important Twenty Seconds*, we know that we can make the transition into seatwork, at least initially, with greater ease. In *Maintaining the Productive Atmosphere: Private Voice and Walking Speed,* we covered two variables that maintain the atmosphere by using a private voice and moving around the room slowly. This skill is a combination of these two.

Mini MITS

Since the teacher's non-verbal communication is the key to management and since the PAUSE is the single most influential non-verbal signal, we have to figure out how to do the pause frequently. Some rules of thumb:

- Every time we use our public teaching voice, we want to do a full *MITS* or at least a *Mini MITS* (e.g., five seconds instead of twenty).

- After every second or third student we assist, stand, breathe and look at the class in general.

To verify these axioms, the teacher will intentionally do the opposite of the recommended way and then do the recommended approach.

Least Recommended

1. During seatwork, intentionally make an announcement and immediately move and help a student. Describe the ripple effect this maneuver has on the class: _____

    _____

    You may want to do this several times to notice the cumulative effect your assignments without a PAUSE have on the class.

2. During this same seatwork time period, make an announcement the recommended way:

    a. Get their attention (remember, speak just above their collective volume then pause and drop your voice).

    b. Make the announcement (drag your voice by slowly emphasizing the words at the end).

    c. PAUSE (full or *Mini MITS*), then slowly help another student.

    Description of a, b and c: _____

    _____

    Description of the effect of 2 compared to 1 above: _____

    _____

Your name _____

Maintaining the Productive Atmosphere
Mini MITS

Stand, Breathe and Look

As you finish helping every second to third student, stand up straight, look around at the class and breathe. The periodic *MITS* (even when we haven't made an announcement) results in the class settling down. There are several factors to consider:

• Are you doing this Stand, Breathe and Look after every, second, third or fourth student? The key is how often does the class need to be settled down.

• Are you facing the class when you Stand, Breathe and Look?

• Are you non-verbally signaling the next student that you will be there in a minute to help her? At times, you will want to cue the student without looking at her. Only touch the student if it is professionally advisable.

Recommended

1. Describe the class signals that you pay attention to in determining the frequency of the maneuver: _____

_____

_____

2. As you did the Stand, Breathe and Look, describe where and how long you were looking: _____

_____

3. Describe how you non-verbally signaled the next student that you would help. Did you decide to look or not look at the student during this time? _____

_____

_____

4. Describe the effects of the above process: did the class settle down, has your stress level decreased and is your energy higher? _____

_____

_____

_____

Mouse Doodles

Be ambitious enough to be patient.
Practice one skill a week.

Antibiotics were finally realized in 1940—30 years after it was first conceived. The heart pacemaker was first conceived in 1928. How long before it was actually realized?

CHAPTER FIVE

eatwork

Chapter Five: Seatwork

"Education is a matter of building a balance between discipline and laxity... between attachment and independence. There is no single prescribed path for creating this equilibrium; and the right measure for one moment (could) be the wrong one for the next."

Lewis Mumford

At those seatwork moments when the room is productively busy, every teacher takes special pride. The atmosphere is so rewarding because needs are being met and independent learning is occurring. It's these snatches that make all our efforts worthwhile. And while you are reveling in it, you pause and think to yourself, "I sure wish I would figure out how to bottle this." This reflection comes because these moments can be so mysteriously ephemeral. This chapter will explore how to increase this productivity. Truthfully, the successful seatwork atmosphere is a result of implementing the Transition to Seatwork skills, *Exit Directions* and *Most Important Twenty Seconds*. So before continuing with the adventures that this chapter holds, be wise enough to have mastered these Transition skillsheets in Chapter One plus those that pertain to Seatwork directly: *OFF/Neutral/ON* and *Influence Approach*.

Motivation

One of the central themes of this chapter is the power of INFLUENCE. When teachers use power to put students ON task, the instructors handcuff themselves by being the motivator for the student's compliant behavior. When teachers use the methods of IN-FLUENCE, we are getting the pupils to think they are the ones motivating themselves. This chapter is subtly questioning some of the undergirding of education. Teachers are a product of a system that has atrophied the right-brain and self-perpetuates left-brain, linear thinking. The historical knee-jerk reaction is to believe that there is actually "system solution" to our classroom ailments; hence, the perennial journey to a pedagogical mecca turns out to be just another short-lived educational fad. The United States has a dropout population of more than twenty-five percent. Every study of the "at risk" shows that from a Learning Style standpoint, the kinesthetic learner and school are incompatible. So what does the "in the trenches" teacher do tomorrow? "Systems" won't affect this population...relationships do!

We could gain a valuable insight by learning from mediators who view conflict as having three levels. The disagreement can be on:

Disagreement Levels

- The issue level
- The needs level
- The relationship level

Disenfranchised Students

The rule of thumb is that if you are at loggerheads on the issue level, then you seek a relationship with the other party. The issue of curriculum for the kinesthetic learner is currently outside the scope of school. These students are disenfranchised because they cannot get their strokes from academic success. As educators, our option is to establish relationships. Once a bond is partially formed, there is a need by both parties to try to maintain the relationship while dealing with the issue. If the relationship is not formed, the teacher has to resort to *Power*. Attempt to keep our purpose of positive contact in mind while learning these skills. These relationship skills take timing. It is worth the practice and effort because the advantage is we are able to use the *Influence Approach*. By implementing these techniques with your marginal students, you will eventually develop the timing needed for your more difficult students.

Sophistication

The following are excellent **Seatwork** skills: *OFF/Neutral/ON Refinements* and the two *Positive Reinforcement: One-on-One* and *Group Feedback. 3 Before Me* is geared for fifth grade and under. This chapter by far has the most sophisticated skills in the whole manual: *Phantom Hand* and "Vacuum Pauses" (it is part of *Power to Influence*). In fact, the full import of these skills can only be appreciated with a seminar or video demonstration. See order form on last page.

Gender Reminder

When applicable, the teacher is referred to with the female pronoun and the student with the male pronoun.

Mouse Doodles

Be ambitious enough to be patient.
Practice one skill a week.

The heart pacemaker was realized in 1960—32 years after it was first conceived. Dry soup mixes were first conceived in 1943. How long before they were finally realized?

Power to Influence Approach

How many Samuels do you have in your room?

Power to Influence Approach

In several other sections, it was suggested that it is best to learn new skills with marginal students because it is easier to practice your timing. With the average student you can use the Indirect approach of Influence to shift a student to appropriate behavior. This section focuses on the "worst case" students. With them, the gentleness of the *Influence Approach* is often too subtle. We are forced to resort to *Power* to get their attention. I am reminded of the story of the gentleman from the city who had saved enough money to buy a weekend farm.

For his first spring in the country he arranged to rent his neighboring farmer's mule to plow some ground for a garden. Bright and early he arose and ate a hearty breakfast. At the appointed hour the neighbor arrived with "Samuel." Having hitched up the beast of burden, the farmer left. Grasping the handles of the plow the city slicker excitedly stood at the head of his future rows of homegrown vegetables. Try as he might, he could not get the mule to move.

Wisdom

After being frustrated for some time, he sought the wisdom of the farmer. The mule's owner asked the gentleman if he had alternated between jerking and slapping the reins on the mule's behind; if he had said, "Giddyup;" if he had stood in front of the mule and tugged on his harness. When the answer to all queries was, "Yes," the farmer paused a brief moment and then silently picked up a two-by-four and walked up to Samuel with the board

hidden. The newcomer dutifully stood at the plow helm while the farmer, looking his animal directly in the eyes, hit him over the head with the lumber.

Help Me Understand

The urbanite was shocked, to say the least, but was immediately pulled along by the mule. Within a much shorter time than expected, the ground was tilled. After returning Samuel to his pen, the still-stunned gardener approached the farmer both to thank him and to ask, "Help me understand your thinking behind what you did!" After scratching his belly twice, the reply was, "Samuel wants to cooperate, and you want to be kind; you just have to get his attention."

As was the case with Samuel, using this approach with the "worst case" students is OK as long as you don't get stuck. We want to use *Power* to shake the student from OFF to Neutral and then do a *Break & Breathe* and shift to the *Influence* approach as we indirectly have the student move from Neutral to ON.

Maintaining Relationships

Once I volunteered to provide inservice to a non-certified inner city preschool. The director arranged for me to shadow her three best teachers and three weakest instructors. The purpose was to determine the difference between the two groups and to give the latter what the former had. The culture and circumstances elicited what, on the surface, was physical grabbing of some students who seemed out of control. At first I thought the less effective teachers did more grabbing with more students than the effective teachers. And while this was true, further observation revealed that the better instructors also had the managed students going ON task more quickly and staying ON task longer. And the real proof was that after a pupil had been disciplined, that student would often, within two minutes, call the teacher over to show her some work that he had proudly done. In other words, the relationship was maintained even though discipline had occurred.

Switching to Influence

I was intrigued that two sets of teachers doing the same interventions were worlds apart in terms of results obtained. After extensive observations, the difference between the two categories of teachers emerged. Both sets of instructors initially did the same thing: *Power* intervention, but the more skilled educators would quickly switch to *Influence*. Two specifics tended to be constant: once the student looked at the teacher and the teacher knew the student was attentive, the teacher would break eye contact and look at the student's work. It was as if the teacher were non-verbally communicating, "You are a good person; it's your behavior I am concerned about!" The second sign of this caring was the way the teacher grabbed the student. If the teacher grabbed the student's elbow, as soon as the pupil looked up at the teacher, the teacher continued to touch the student's elbow but the student had full latitude of movement of the arm and posture. The teacher's hand and the student's elbow were like dance partners. The teacher initially led with a jerk to shake the student from his fantasy world of being OFF task to Neutral and then let the student lead himself into being ON task.

Patience

Because of the sophistication of these skills, we ask the reader to be ambitious enough to have completed the following sections before proceeding with this one.

- *OFF/Neutral/ON*, both self and peer forms.

- *Influence Approach*, both self and peer forms.

- *Decontamination of the Classroom*, self form.

- *Break & Breathe*, self form.

By doing the above-mentioned prerequisite exercises, the practitioner will have knowledge and ability to do the following skills:

- recognition of OFF vs. Neutral vs. ON task.

- the difference between
  Power = Direct vs.
  Influence = Indirect.

- sorting mental states by locations.

- the role of breathing in all of the above.

Power to Influence Approach

Overview

We are presuming that the indirect approach wasn't effective. The extreme right-brain kinesthetic student is a member of the ESP Club = Earth as a Second Planet. If we approach too subtly, the student remains gone. Therefore, we are going to do the *Power to Influence Approach*. You will be using some or all of the non-verbal components of the direct approach of *Power*.

Power Approach

- Teacher approaches from front

- Teacher makes eye contact

- Teacher is breathing high and shallow

- Teacher is close, perhaps touching the student

- Teacher is verbal, perhaps using a loud voice

Influence Approach

- Moving to the student's side

- Looking at the work on the student's desk

- Breathing low and full

- Being farther away

- Either using no voice or a whisper

This switch from a disciplinarian to a teaching persona is basically what we did when we practiced *ABOVE (Pause) Whisper*.

You will, of course, be doing one continuous intervention while the questions that follow delineate the stages separately.

Once you have the student's attention (the pupil is in Neutral), you want to change to the indirect approach of *Influence*. We do this by deleting any non-verbal signals that are person-to-person. This includes stopping any eye contact, high and shallow breathing, harsh touch or loud voice, etc. Instead, we change to a person-to-content emphasis.

Your name _____

Power to Influence Approach

First Example

1. Initials of a worst case student: _____

2. Approach the student indirectly and describe what happens: _____
_____

3. Describe which aspects of the *Power Approach* you used: _____
_____

   Describe what you noticed that indicated that the student had come back to earth and was in a Neutral state so that the teacher could stop the *Power Approach*: _____
_____

   Describe your *Break & Breathe:* _____

4. Describe which aspects of the *Influence Approach* you used: _____
_____

5. Describe the beneficial results for you and the student: _____
_____

Second Example

1. Initials of another worst case student: _____

2. Approach the student indirectly and describe what happened: _____
_____

3. Describe which aspects of the *Power Approach* you used: _____
_____

   Describe what you noticed that indicated that the student had come back to earth and was in a Neutral state so the teacher could stop the *Power Approach*: _____
_____

   Describe your *Break & Breathe*: _____

4. Describe which aspects of the *Influence Approach* you used: _____
_____

5. Describe the beneficial results for yourself and the student: _____
_____

Power to Influence Approach

Observational Skills

What you are about to do is a very subtle, yet powerful skill. You are going to learn about and practice timing. This skill will take patience on your part and a commitment to practice observational abilities. I am reminded of the correspondence between Dr. Livingston in Africa and a colleague back in Great Britain. The former received from the latter a letter stating, "Have you made a trail—we have scientists to send." Livingston replied, "If they need a trail, don't send them!"

The "worst case" students are often labeled hyperactive. Because they have difficulty remaining focused, the teacher is managing and redirecting these students. A possible description of their behaviors might include:

Hyperactive Characteristics
- impulsive and very, very quick.
- concentration spans are extremely short.
- don't focus well or long.
- above average intelligence.
- externally oriented, with high distractibility tendencies.

Because of these propensities, they don't stay OFF task, on the same thing long, nor ON task long. They are like a fly that randomly buzzes from noticing one external object to another. By filling out the form on the next page, you will practice noticing this distractibility pattern.

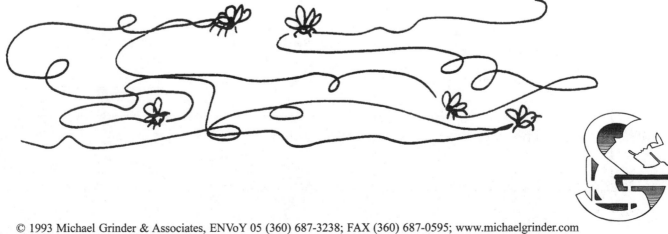

Your name _____

Power to Influence Approach

Inventory In Another's Room

l. Sit in a classroom where you are not responsible for the conduct of the students or the pace of the learning. This is most easily done when you visit someone else's room. Select a student who is really in his own world. List initials of student or physical description of his clothing or seat location: _____. Kinesthetic learners have a strong fantasy world. Have a watch with a second hand. For one to two minutes, observe the selected student and put a check every time the student mentally shifts us from one internal or external focus to another.

_____ , _____ , _____ , _____ , _____ , _____ ,

_____ , _____ , _____ , _____ , _____ , _____ ,

_____ , _____ , _____ , _____ , _____ , _____ ,

_____ , _____ , _____ , _____ , _____ , _____ .

2. You are practicing seeing the external signs of a student who had one focus, then had a brief "**vacuum pause**," then another focus. Now that you know what you are looking for, do another student. Initials or description: _____

_____ , _____ , _____ , _____ , _____ , _____ ,

_____ , _____ , _____ , _____ , _____ , _____ ,

_____ , _____ , _____ , _____ , _____ , _____ ,

_____ , _____ , _____ , _____ , _____ , _____ .

3. Stop recording and just notice the gap between when the student finishes focusing on one thing and before the student focuses on the next thing. This gap is like a vacuum pause. Nothing is happening. The student is in a limbo state; he is in a temporary Neutral. Write what you are noticing about this student's vacuum pause. Describe what you see the student's body doing during the student's vacuum pause.

_____

_____

_____

_____

_____

Your name _____

Power to Influence Approach

Intervening at the Vacuum Pause

Since a teacher often has to do a two-step intervention, getting the student from OFF to Neutral and from Neutral to ON, intervening during a vacuum pause—an innate Neutral—saves a step.

Our goal is to intervene at the vacuum pause. This can be done visually (e.g., catch the student's eyes), through the auditory mode (e.g., say the student's name or clear your throat) or kinesthetically (move toward the student or touch). The difficulty is that when we see the student in a vacuum pause and then start to intervene, by the time we actually do the intervention, enough time has elapsed so that the student is no longer at the vacuum pause but now is OFF task on a new focus. We literally missed the vacuum pause between the time gap of "when we saw" and "when we did." Therefore, we need to notice the rhythm or frequency of the length between the vacuum pause and the next OFF task focus.

Timing

Each student has a given frequency as to how often the vacuum pause comes. Also, he usually shows indicators at the end of one focus so that you can anticipate that the vacuum pause is coming. This allows you to start your intervention (e.g., look at, say name, touch, etc.) toward the end of one focus. By the time you do the intervention, you are at his vacuum pause.

Observe two students. They can be the same ones you watched on the previous page or two different students. Make up a code that you can use to record when you see the signs of the vacuum pause (e.g., a check) and when you see the signs of indicating that a focus was coming to an end (e.g., a dash):

First student's initials or description of:_____

Code: _____

_____

_____

Second student's initials or description of: _____

Code: _____

_____

_____

Power to Influence Approach

In Your Own Room

Now that you have practiced seeing indicators that a vacuum pause is coming, pick two students in your own room who are often really OFF task. Attempt to do interventions. What is great about practicing this skill is that even if you aim for a vacuum pause and instead get a focus, you learn about timing. As with most perceptual training, there is no failure, only feedback. When you intervene at a vacuum pause, you will be convinced of the effectiveness of timing and therefore be motivated to continue to practice.

Your name _____

Power to Influence Approach

Power Intervening

First student's initials: _____

    Description of attempt(s): What were the signs that you keyed on to know when to attempt the intervention(s) and what were the results? _____

_____

_____

_____

_____

Second student's initials: _____

    Description of attempt(s): What were the signs that you keyed on to know when to attempt the intervention(s) and what were the results? _____

_____

_____

_____

Switching to Influence

    Whether you increase your consistency of intervening at the student's vacuum point or not, in either case we have shifted the student from OFF task to neutral because at this point we want to change from the Power Approach (direct) to the Influence Approach (indirect). Describe what your non-verbal signals were during the Power Approach as you shifted the student from OFF to Neutral and what they were during the Influence Approach as you shifted the student from Neutral to ON:

First student: _____

_____

_____

_____

Second student: _____

_____

_____

_____

OFF/Neutral/ON Refinements

???
??   "Fundamental to the teacher's credo is the belief that all   ??
??   students **can** learn. Furthermore, they act on that belief."   ??
??   National Board for Professional Teaching Standards   ??
??   ??
???

Respectful Weeping Optional

Paradigm Shift

The skill you are about to read will be the most controversial ENVoY concept. While we believe that "all students can learn," many educational systems **cannot** financially provide what is needed to act on that credo. *OFF/Neutral/ON Refinement* will offer a paradigm shift.

Your name _____

OFF/Neutral/ON Refinements

The two major concepts from which all our **Seatwork** skills have evolved are

- the *Influence Approach,*

- making sure they are ON task as you leave them.

For the refinements, we will cover two concepts: Dot-to-Dot and Two Stage Exiting.

Dot-to-Dot

On days when we feel like we are chasing our tails, we are trying to handle the seatwork productivity in a manner that can be labeled "dot-to-dot." Remember as a child the drawing books with blank pages except for numbers with dots next to them? We would trace from one number's dot to the next. Well, on days that we are frantic, we tend to race around from one student who is OFF task to another. If we had a video camera centered on the classroom ceiling and reviewed the tape at the fast forward speed, we could see ourselves going dot-to-dot with certain students. The difference between the drawing book and this video is that the former made a picture that made sense.

Inventory

At this time, it is suggested that you have the observer come in and fill out the Inventory section from the peer form (page 231).

1. For two days, notice those students you helped one-on-one during seatwork at least twice in a ten-minute period. List their initials here: _____, _____ , _____, _____, _____, _____ and _____.

2. During this same two days, notice which students you attempted to put on task at least twice in a ten-minute period. List their initials here: _____, _____, _____, _____, _____, _____ and _____.

One way to accomplish numbers 1 and 2 is to use a seating chart. Every time you **help** a student, put an "H" next to the student's initials. Every time you **manage** a student on task, record an "M" next to the student's initials.

3. Look at the two lists.

- Which students just appear on the first list? List their initials here: _____, _____, _____, _____. We will designate these students Group H—those you Help.

- Which students appear on both lists? List their initials here: _____, _____, _____, _____. These students will be designated Group H & M—those you both Help and Manage.

- Which students appear on only the second list? List their initials here: _____, _____, _____, _____. These students will be designated Group M—students who you mainly have contact with by managing them.

OFF/Neutral/ON Refinements

Suggestions

You will know your circumstances much better than any generalized theory, so as you read the following suggestions, temper them to suit your situation. You may want to invite the observer in after you practice the skills associated with each of the three categories of students. Make sure you read the directions for the corresponding form in Chapter 10 because sometimes the wording is different than on the form you are filling out.

Group H

The students you can help one-on-one. This is the classification of students we all want to help.

Invite the observer in to give you feedback about yourself in regard to these students. Make sure you read the peer form section on "Suggestions" and "Group H." There you will find the debriefing questions that the observer will ask you.

Group H & M

Pay particular attention to this group that you spend time putting back ON task and can help one-on-one. Notice if there is a correlation between when you have helped them and when they increase their ON-task behavior. In other words, are they misbehaving because they are unable to academically involve themselves? If so, the teacher won't attempt the *Influence Approach* because it won't work. Instead, the teacher will go directly over and help them as soon as possible after she has released the class to do seatwork *(Exit Directions* and *MITS)*. If the teacher cannot go, she will try not to expect compliance. The teacher will consider that the students in question are temporarily in Group M. If the students are not bothering others and you don't have time to help them, let the students be. Reflect on how you are handling these students and what effect this new approach is having

Group M

These are the pupils that you primarily have contact with through management rather than by helping them. Reflect on how much you are managing them:

- for their own good

- or because their off-task behaviors are interfering with others' learning

For those you answered with "for their own good," ask yourself how effectively your time and energy is being utilized compared to the time spent with Groups H and H & M students. Our profession is famous for doing things because of a philosophical consideration that we believe in, even if it is less than effective. It is not that we plan to ignore Group M students, it is just that they have the last number in the educational service line. By making the distinction between Group M students who are bothering others and those who are not, summarize the change in your own self-esteem and the productive use of your time during seat work.

OFF/Neutral/ON Refinements

Summary of dot-to-dot

You have categorized some of the pupils into three groups:

- Group H—students you help

- Group H & M—students whom you both help and manage

- Group M—students whom you mainly manage

Your purpose in practicing these skills is to prevent racing around the room in a dot-to-dot fashion. As educators, we have a limited amount of time and energy during seatwork. We have to prioritize. The suggestions have been to help Group H and H & M students and to distinguish between those students in Group M who ARE INTERFERING WITH OTHERS' LEARNING and those students who are not ON task but are not bothering others. For the former, intervene; with the latter, leave them alone unless you have the time. What are you noticing about your learning from practicing these suggestions?

Reflection

Sometimes it is so frustrating that we can't do what we love to do—teach. A very wise veteran educator once remarked, "We don't often get to be as good as we are capable of being." If I understand what he meant, he was saying that, as a group, teachers are perceived as the second most giving professionals there are. That's why Christa McAuliffe was selected as the first civilian to fly in outer space. We love to impart, assist, facilitate others. Of course, this whole *ENVoY* book is intended to make us more effective in our management skills so that we can spend more time giving. The suggestion is to notice how you feel toward the students. For most of us, our heart goes out to them. Now ask yourself what may seem like an odd question: How do you feel about your feelings toward Group H & M students? In other words, how are you able to accept that you are part of a system that often cannot sufficiently serve these pupils. The more realistically we can view our range of influence, the more we take pride in what we can do, resulting in our having higher motivation. Reflect on your level of acceptance and motivation and what it would take to increase both.

Pair "A" Dimes Shift

Your name _____

OFF/Neutral/ON Refinements

Two Stage Exiting

OFF/Neutral/ON and *Influence Approach* focus on getting a student from OFF task through Neutral to ON task. Using these skills will change the syndrome of negative contact between the teacher and the at-risk student to positive contact. Now a new problem arises: how to get away from the student. This stems from two causes. Sometimes the student is "contact hungry" and doesn't want the teacher to leave and sometimes our presence is needed to keep him ON task. In either case, the following skill will be of assistance.

When the student has been ON task for at least two breaths (the pupil has inhaled and exhaled twice):

1. Slowly position your body so that you are standing upright and next to the student.

2. Since eye contact in a positive situation will usually increase the personal contact of the interaction and thereby elicit an interchange, keep your eyes on the student's work. This completes the first stage of exiting.

3. Slowly and gradually step back from the student so that the student cannot see you. Watch the student to make sure the pupil does remain ON task independent of you.

4. Slowly and gradually move away from the student.

The numbers below correspond to those immediately above.

First Student

Initials of a student you want to practice this skill with: _____

1. Describe how long it took to position yourself in an upright position and what it was you saw that indicated the student was breathing fully and was ON task: _____

_____

2. Describe how you kept your eyes on the student's work: _____

_____

3. Describe how you slowly and gradually stepped back from the student so the student couldn't easily see you and mention how the student stayed on task without you there. Also mention how long it took and if you had to do any modification because certain conditions occurred: _____

_____

4. You are now standing behind the student, describe how you slowly and gradually moved away from the student and the student stayed on task. Also, mention how long it took and if you had to do any modification because certain conditions occurred: _____

_____

Your name _____

OFF/Neutral/On Refinements

Second Student

Initials of a student you want to practice this with: _____

1. Describe how long it took to position yourself in an upright position and what it was you saw that indicated he was breathing fully and was ON task: _____

_____

2. Describe how you kept your eyes on the student's work: _____

_____

3. Describe how you slowly and gradually stepped back from the student so the student couldn't easily see you and mention how the student stayed on task. Also mention how long it took and if you had to do any modification because certain conditions occurred:

_____

4. You are now standing behind the student, describe how you slowly and gradually moved away from the student and the student stayed on task. Also, mention how long it took and if you had to do any modification because certain conditions occurred: _____

_____

OFF/Neutral/ON Refinements Summary

Having practiced the skills of vacuum pause and two stage exiting separately, now combine these skills:

*   Intervene with the *Power Approach*.

*   When the student is in Neutral, switch to the *Influence Approach*.

*   When the student is ON task, slowly and gradually step back from the student.

*   Slowly and gradually move away from the student.

Positive Reinforcement: One-on-One

A poet once said, "Children will get our attention. The only question is whether the contact will be positive or not. The answer depends on how soon and how often we give the attention."

Your name _____

Positive Reinforcement: One-on-One

A survey of educators indicates that teachers are more "people oriented" than "idea oriented." Research shows that their energy level is higher and their self-image greater when they give students "positive strokes." Conversely, their energy level and self-image decrease when they discipline. It is obvious that methods that increase the teacher's use of Positive Reinforcement and decrease Negative Reinforcement are most welcome.

Length of Time

Often the difference between a stroke and a reprimand is the *length of time* between strokes. For example, during seatwork the teacher is at the transparency projector calling students up to demonstrate ability on the overhead screen. The teacher has judiciously placed Sam (a highly kinesthetic student) in the front row to keep him ON task. The teacher does a variety of techniques to interrupt his inappropriate behavior and put him back ON task. The teacher is using a disciplinary response. For about 30 to 40 seconds, Sam stays ON task. The teacher is intervening every 60 to 90 seconds. If the teacher gives positive strokes every 25 seconds, the length of time the student will stay ON task often increases and the teacher feels better using positive actions.

Stroking

Another way of looking at switching from negative interaction (disciplining) to positive interaction (stroking) is each time the teacher does disciplinary intervention, she follows with visual, auditory or kinesthetic praise within 20 to 25 seconds. This assures the teacher that the student knows what behavior the teacher wants and that the student can get attention in a positive way.

This concept is especially true for right-brain students because of these traits:

Right Brain Students

- Person to person interaction
- Short attention span
- Distractibility
- Need for immediate reinforcement

Positive Reinforcement: One-on-One

The following exercises will help you practice this concept. It is recommended that you practice this skill on a marginal student.

First Student

Initials of a marginal student: _____

1. Describe the student's inappropriate behavior: _____

_____

_____

_____

2. Do your normal process of disciplinary intervention.

   • How often did you do it (e.g., "every _____ seconds or minutes") _____

   • How long does the student stay on task? _____

   _____

   _____

3. Now practice this *Positive Reinforcement* technique. Initially do your normal process of disciplinary intervention. Then, while the student is still ON task, praise the student for appropriate behavior.

   • How did you know you could wait as long as you did? In other words, what were the indications the student was still ON task but nearing the end of his concentration?

   _____

   _____

   _____

   • What was your praise or positive reinforcement? Keep in mind that sometimes non-verbal reinforcements are better than verbal ones: _____

   _____

   _____

4. Briefly describe the results. Especially notice if the length of the student's ON task behavior increases. _____

_____

_____

Your name _____

Positive Reinforcement: One-on-One

Second Student

Initials of another marginal student: _____

1. Describe a student's inappropriate behavior: _____

_____

_____

2. Do your normal process of disciplinary intervention.

   •   How often did you do it (e.g., "every _____ seconds or minutes")?_____

   •   How long does the student stay ON task? _____

_____

_____

3. Now practice this *Positive Reinforcement* technique. Initially do your normal process of disciplinary intervention. Then, while the student is still ON task, praise the student for appropriate behavior.

   •   How did you know you could wait as long as you did? In other words, what were the indications the student was still ON task but nearing the end of his concentration?

_____

_____

_____

   •   What was your praise or positive reinforcement? Keep in mind that sometimes non-verbal reinforcements are better than verbal ones: _____

_____

_____

_____

4. Briefly describe the results. Especially notice if the length of the student's ON task behavior increases. _____

_____

_____

_____

Positive Reinforcement: Group Feedback

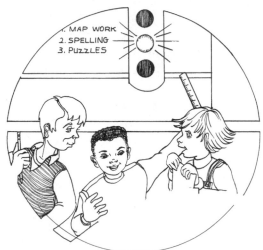

As teachers, we espouse our desire for students to be autonomous. If we verbally give the class feedback, they are dependent on a source outside themselves on how they are doing. The following skill allows the pupils to receive feedback when they are starting to wander from the acceptable norm and allows them to correct themselves.

There are two ingredients of fairness:

- that the teacher is consistent

- that the students know **it** is coming

Group Feedback directly addresses the second component. We all want to be fair.

(See page 145 for details of an actual classroom stoplight.)

Positive Reinforcement: Group Feedback

Seatwork time is most productive when the students are both ON task and relaxed. If some of the students are other than appropriate, we need to give them feedback as to what we expect and how they are doing compared to those expectations. If we give this feedback orally, we become the "traffic cop." While this may increase their productivity, we have used the *Power Approach*, which means among other things that they are not relaxed. We also have increased the likelihood that they perceive that they need to be ON task for us instead of thinking they are self-motivated. We may need to stay visibly present and therefore cannot go help students one-on-one.

In the section, *Positive Reinforcement: One-on-One*, the age-old concept of "catch 'em doing it right" was explored for the one-on-one situations. Applied here, we want to collectively give students positive strokes while they are still ON task but are starting to fade and at the same time we would like to use the *Influence Approach*. There are many by-products of this method. They think they are motivating themselves, we get to still help students one-on-one and they are relaxed. We can accomplish giving feedback in silence with visual non-verbal signals. The examples given work well through fourth grade and have to be somewhat modified for the middle grades and greatly altered for high school.

Stoplight

The teacher has had the high school wood shop use electrical light sockets and red, yellow and green light bulbs to make her a traffic signal device. When the students are doing well, the green light is on. If they start to become other than appropriate, the green light is turned off and the yellow light is turned on. This Myrtle Creek, Oregon, self-contained fifth-grade teacher reports that nine out of ten times the students immediately return to appropriate behavior. After they have settled down, she leaves the yellow light on for one to two more minutes and then quietly turns the yellow light off and the green light back on. When she was asked what happens when the red light comes on, with a chuckle she replied, "Oh, you don't want to know." She also mentioned that she replaces green light bulbs several times a year and hasn't bought a yellow or red one since she started the process five years ago.

R E C E S S

Kathy Force is a third-grade teacher who has six separate cards off to the right of the chalkboard held up with Velcro on the back. Each card has a letter on it. The cards collectively spell out R E C E S S. If the class is other than appropriate, the last letter is turned sideways. If their behavior continues, then the letter is taken away - which symbolizes that they have lost one minute of recess. The process is negative reinforcement but an excellent visual feedback system. This approach is often ideal for our right-brain sections of the school years, e.g., the week before winter vacation. Kathy uses other systems for her positive reinforcements for the regular weeks of the year.

Your name _____

Positive Reinforcement: Group Feedback

Barometer

The instructor is a media center teacher for an elementary school. This is an important consideration because "specialists" on the elementary level act more like secondary educators because both groups are not self-contained and therefore the management styles are different than those who teach in self-contained classrooms. The teacher has used tag board to make a half circle that looks like a setting sun. The half circle is divided into four sections. The far left is green, the next is a faded combination of green and yellow, the next section is yellow and the far right is red. On the bottom in the center a brad holds a pointer that can be rotated into any section. The pointer is pointed straight down when the system is not in use. It functions much like the traffic light in Stoplight example. The students have constant feedback on how they are doing. Green = super, green-yellow = fading, yellow = caution, red = penalty.

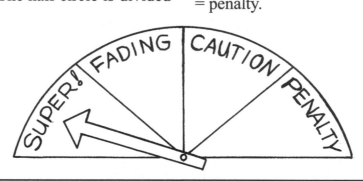

In the examples above, the educators are attempting to provide silent visual feedback that can be used to positively reinforce the desired behavior you want.

1. Describe your new visual feedback system plan: _____

_____

_____

_____

_____

2. Is its effect different from your previous system? Especially mention the advantages of this new *Influence Approach*: _____

_____

_____

_____

_____

Mouse Doodles

Be ambitious enough to be patient.
Practice one skill a week.

Dry soup mixes were finally realized in 1962—19 years after they were first conceived. Roll-on deodorant was first conceived in 1948. How many years before it was realized?

Here are two devices that provide the class feedback—ideal for self-monitoring.

Teach Timer

An indispensable "time management tool" for trainers, teachers and students.

Teach Timers were specifically designed for the classroom teacher to use in timing tests, reading assignments, science experiments or any other classroom or school activity.

When placed on the stage of any standard overhead projector, Teach Timers project in large numerals the amount of minutes/seconds remaining during timed events. A pre-alarm warning feature lets you set a warning of 0, 1, 2, 3, 4, or 5 minutes before time set for activity is to expire. The Teach Timer can also be placed on a desktop in a stand-up position for personal or small group viewing.

Yacker Tracker

Traffic light is computerized with adjustable sound level meter which can be set from 40 dB to 120 dB. Green light stays lit until noise in room goes above set level, then a flashing yellow light comes on as a warning. When sound level reaches 20 decibels above set level, a red light and siren sound come on (siren sound is optional). Unit is 16 " tall and can stand on its own or be mounted on the wall. AC powered.

See advertisements on pages 274-278.

3 Before Me

3 Before Me is an example of systematically using non-verbal signals to communicate complicated skills. Any message we say on a repetitive basis is a candidate for a poster that explains the routine. You will love the time you save!

In the above example, a student approaches a teacher. The teacher signals with three fingers, "Have you checked (1) the board, (2) the assignment sheet, and (3) with a tablemate?" The student signals back that he has. The teacher finishes helping the girl and then helps the boy.

Your name _____

3 Before Me

(My thanks to Peter Bellamy of Carus School)

We know that the best productive environment for seatwork is a "visual" atmosphere and management that is done with a maximum of non-verbal communication. It all begins with the directions being given on the board visually. We also know that seatwork is the time when the teacher can work individually with students. This skill focuses on how to increase students' independence in what they do. They will have less need to interrupt you, and you will be more able to choose which students you want to help. This skill is designed for students from kindergarten through fifth grade. It would need to be modified for older students.

Make a poster that has the title: *3 Before Me*. Then list the three things that the students have to do before asking you. Some suggestions are:

---

3 Before Me

1. Check the board.

2. Check the assignment sheet.

3. Check with a table mate.

---

3 Before Me

1. Look at the schedule.

2. Remember what was said.

3. Ask a neighbor.

---

1. What is your *3 Before Me*? _____

2. Now create a non-verbal signal that you can quickly and respectfully use when a student approaches you. For example, as the student nears you, you could hold up 3 fingers and gently shrug your shoulders to mimic a question. That way, the students are encouraged to reflect. What is your non-verbal signal? _____

Make sure you rehearse the non-verbal signal with the class.

3. Create a non-verbal signal that the students can show as they approach you. This saves you doing number 2 above and indicates they have already done the reflection. For example, they could approach you with their 3 fingers already held up. What is the non-verbal signal they can show? _____

_____

Variation

As the student approaches, some teachers use a hand gesture to indicate "stop" (like a traffic cop directing traffic). The student can override the stop sign and indicate there is an emergency by placing his hand in a horizontal position on top of the teacher's vertical hand. This forms the letter "T" which represents "time out/emergency."

Phantom Hand

We all have had the experience of putting an infant to sleep in our arms. The child doesn't want us to leave. The challenge is how to make the transition of putting the baby down without waking the baby up. By making the transition slowly enough, the child will "phantomly" think we are still there. This also applies when we want to get out of bed in the morning and not disturb our spouses. By systematically doing the transition, our spouses peacefully sleep as if we were still there. So, too, in our classrooms, there are ways of leaving a student who is ON task and still have the pupil sense our presence.

Phantom Hand is a four step process.

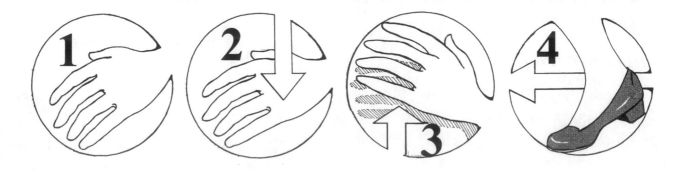

Phantom Hand

We know that a kinesthetic student often operates as if he needs our presence to stay on task during seatwork. As much as the student wants to have individual "papal visits," we need to assist and monitor all of our students. The question arises, "How do we make our presence known from a distance?"

In answer to this question we are presuming the reader has done *Influence Approach* and that you know how to approach a student when he is ON task so that your presence is a "positive contact." This skill is designed to refine your ability to leave the student with the positive contact and still have your presence felt after you leave.

There are four stages to the *Phantom Hand*:

- Increase Touch
- Decrease Touch
- Lift Off
- Exiting

Because of the sophistication of this technique, you and a colleague will want to read the description of the four stages together, then role play the skill. In this situation the student has been OFF task and you have approached indirectly. As you stopped at an adjacent student, the selected student has gone ON task (see *OFF/Neutral/ON* and *Influence Approach* for more details).

Increase Touch

a. "Original Touch:" You are standing at the student's side (whether or not you have talked or looked at the student) and are ready to leave. You are touching the student (always be professional—we are assuming for this situation you have permission and it is appropriate to touch). Your fingers are spread out and contoured to the student's shoulder. Have the student move his shoulder so that you can practice your arm being in unison with the student's movement. It is like a dance; the student has *full range of mobility* and your hand is following it. You are getting ready to exit from the student; therefore, you are looking at the student's work and are preferably silent.

b. "Initial Increase:" Increase your hand's pressure just a little; make sure it is well within the student's comfort zone. The increase is not an increase in grip...the fingers and thumb are not moving toward each other; instead, the weight of contact is being felt and increased.

c. "Additional Increase:" Do an additional increase in the pressure; still well within the student's comfort zone and he still has *full mobility.*

Phantom Hand

Decrease Touch

Keeping your torso and, especially, your feet still, look at the student's work and do Decrease Touch:

a. Take five seconds to decrease from "additional increase" to the "initial increase" (returning to "Increase Touch").

b. Take five seconds to decrease from the "initial increase" to the "original touch."

c. Take five seconds to go from the "original touch" to barely touching.

Lift Off

a. Take five seconds to move your hand from barely touching to being within half inch of the contact point of the student.

b. Take five seconds to move your hand from half inch to a foot away from contact point.

c. Take five seconds to move your hand from a foot away from contact point to your hand being at your side.

During stages two and three, keep your torso and, especially, your feet still and look at the student's work.

Exiting

Slowly exit away so the student can't easily see you.

KEEP YOUR FEET & TORSO STILL.

Your name _____

Phantom Hand

Practice With A Colleague

When the word, "student," appears, it is referring to the peer who is role playing the student.

1. Description of how you got this student from OFF to ON task: _____

_____

_____

2. Did you keep your torso and, especially, your feet still while looking at the student's work? _____

3. Check off that you did:

Increase Touch

_____ original touch with fingers spread.

_____ initial increase.

_____ additional increase.

Decrease Touch

_____ decrease from "additional increase" back to the "initial increase" level of contact.

_____ decrease from "initial increase" back to the "original touch" level of contact.

_____ *g r a d u a l l y* lift hand from contact to barely touching.

Lift Off

_____ *g r a d u a l l y* lift hand from barely touching to being half inch from contact.

_____ *g r a d u a l l y* lift hand from half inch to a foot away from contact point.

_____ *g r a d u a l l y* drop your hand to your side.

Exiting

_____ *s l o w l y* exit from student so he cannot see you.

Debrief with your colleague who has been role-playing the student. Ask him if he felt as if the hand were still there. Discuss the implementation. We need to leave the student to help others and yet we want to leave the pupil ON task by having our presence felt after we leave. By doing the four stages, we achieve the influence of our presence with the *Phantom Hand*. Make sure you and your colleague switch roles so you both get to experience the sensation of the *Phantom Hand*.

Your name _____

Phantom Hand

Practicing In Your Classroom

We want to be mindful of the two prerequisites of being an effective manager: we have a relationship with the student in question and the student can be successful with the curriculum. Therefore, we want to practice this skill with a marginal student rather than an at-risk student. You may want to reread the discussion about Group H, Group H & M and Group M students (*OFF/Neutral/On Refinements*).

1. Initials of a marginal student: _____

2. Description of how you got this student from OFF to ON task: _____

_____

3. Did you keep your torso and, especially, your feet still while looking at the student's work? _____

4. Check off that you did:

Increase Touch

_____ original touch with fingers spread.

_____ initial increase.

_____ additional increase.

Decrease Touch

_____ decrease from "additional increase" back to the "initial increase" level of contact.

_____ decrease from "initial increase" back to the "original touch" level of contact.

_____ *g r a d u a l l y* lift hand from contact to barely touching.

Lift Off

_____ *g r a d u a l l y* lift hand from barely touching to being half inch from contact.

_____ *g r a d u a l l y* lift hand from half inch to a foot away from contact point.

_____ *g r a d u a l l y* drop your hand to your side.

Exiting

_____ *s l o w l y* exit from student so that he cannot see you.

Description of the results of 1 - 4: _____

_____

Your name _____

Phantom Hand

With A Colleague

Least Recommended

Because of the subtlety of this technique, we recommend you do the "Doing It Wrong" steps. There are basically three ways that we inadvertently miss doing the *Phantom Hand*. For each of these ineffective ways, make sure the teacher has correctly done the first stage of "Increase Touch." First practice this skill with a colleague.

• Pat the student's back as you move your feet and leave. We call this "baby burping." This definitely gives the sensation that the teacher has left.

• Pretend again that you are at the end of "Increase Touch" and rub your hand as you move your feet and leave. Another way of doing this is "wiping off" the contact point. That is, if the teacher was touching the student's shoulder, let your hand fall all the way down the student's back as you leave.

• Pretend again that you are at the end of "Increase Touch" and move your feet while withdrawing your hand.

• Make sure you and your colleague both role-play the student and teacher parts of these three ineffective ways of removing contact.

With A Student

Least Recommended

You may want to actually do the less effective format with a student to experience the contrast from the suggested format.

1. Initials of one a marginal student: _____

    Have the student at the end of "Increase Touch." Check off which of the following three less effective formats you did:

    _____ "Baby burping."

    _____ "Wipe off."

    _____ Simultaneous release of hand while leaving.

2. Describe the results, e.g., how long did the student stay ON task compared to the recommended format: _____

    _____

    _____

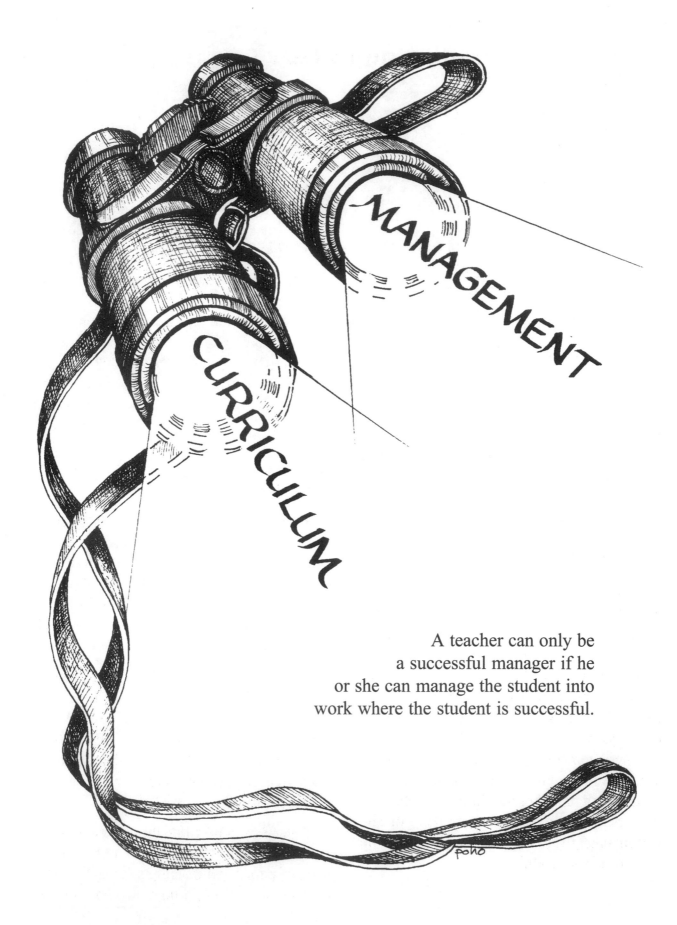

A teacher can only be
a successful manager if he
or she can manage the student into
work where the student is successful.

Introduction to Peer Forms

"It is patently foolish to expect individual teachers to learn and apply the ideas of current research on teaching by themselves."

Dr. Richard Elmore
Harvard University
Graduate School of Education

ENVoY is a vehicle to shift educators from seeing themselves as bastions of power to instruments of influence. This program, when used by cadres of instructors within a school, brings out the professional strengths of all members involved. We need to elevate ourselves from within...we need systems which enable us to profit from the wealth of abilities that lie in insular classrooms. It is only through sharing and supporting processes that the collective wisdom of the staff emerges.

Guidelines

Curriculum

As a coach, once in awhile there may be a visitation where the teacher is doing the specific skillsheet quite well and yet you are concerned. You wonder whether your colleague might profit more from a different focus for his or her professional development. The classroom can be viewed with educational binoculars. ENVoY focuses on the management aspects of the learning environment. Equally important is the other educational tube—curriculum. A teacher can only be a successful manager if he or she can manage the student into work where the student is successful.

Volunteerism

Hopefully, the reader is fortunate enough to be a member of a cadre of teachers at the same school who are joined in supporting each other's professional development through ENVoY. The teacher being observed always selects the skills and invites the peer into the classroom. We assume that when you are filling out forms from Chapters Six through Ten, you have a high degree of familiarity because you have completed your own "self forms."

When you are invited to fill out an observer form from Chapters Seven through Ten, it may not be one you are familiar with; hopefully, the condensed information on the observer form will be sufficient to produce a meaningful observation. If not, then read and, perhaps, do the corresponding self form.

PLEASE NOTE: IT IS THE RESPONSIBILITY OF THE TEACHER BEING OBSERVED TO ARRANGE THE CLASSROOM ACTIVITY SO THAT THE FOCUS OF THE VISIT CAN BE SEEN. In most cases, five to fifteen minutes is sufficient for the observation.

Several of us may find the enclosed forms not to our liking. Feel free to use a blank piece of paper and develop your own code. Remember that our purpose is to provide the teacher feedback; therefore, make sure your format makes sense to the teacher.

In addition to teachers being the observer for the peer forms, most forms can be completed by classified staff, parent volunteers and, in some cases, students.

Benefits to Observer

When you observe, in many ways your insights regarding your own classroom management will become clearer than when you are practicing the ENVoY skills on your own -why? When we are in our own classroom, our level of responsibility is much higher than when we are in a colleague's room. While teaching, we are focused on content; whereas, ENVoY is an emphasis on process. In our own room, educationally we cannot see the "process forest through the content trees."

Guidelines to Coaches

If you are asked by an administrator to assist a teacher with classroom management skills, remember that the strength of any peer coaching program is the volunteerism. Acknowledge the administrator's commitment to helping a staff member with that teacher's professional development, then politely mention to the administrator that you would be willing to explore the possibility of assisting the teacher in question. The most effective way to be of assistance is for the administrator to ask the teacher in question to initiate a conversation with you. Be clear with the supervisor that all observation information and forms are the confidential property of the teacher, not the administrator or observer. See pages 266-268 in the Appendix for the forms that administrators use with a teacher.

Least Recommended vs. Recommended

The **ENVoY** manual often suggests that the teacher do the least recommended way and then do the recommended maneuver. This contrasting approach encourages the teacher to discover what methods work for that teacher. As a coach, if the teacher only wants to do the recommended way, respect the teacher's decision.

Self vs. Peer Form

When you are asked to observe, remember that your function as a coach is to assist the teacher to empower him or herself. You would only use the peer forms after the teacher has successfully completed the self form. If the teacher hasn't done so, do a visitation and help the teacher fill out the self form. Some of the peer forms are designed so that volunteers, classified and some students above third grade can complete them.

Progression of Skills Observed

We advise that the teacher learn the ENVoY skills in this progression:

* All skills in Chapters Two through Five stem from the skills in Chapter One; therefore, when learning a Chapter Two through Five skill, learn the Chapter One skill that is associated with that phase. For example, in the phase, Getting Their Attention, the teacher would need to learn *Freeze Body* and *ABOVE (Pause)*

Whisper from Chapter One before practicing any of the Chapter Two skills.

- Fill out a self form.

- Give a colleague a corresponding peer form and ask the colleague to do an observation.

- Do all of the skills you are interested in in a given chapter.

- Continue to do the format of doing a self form and having a colleague do the corresponding peer form until you have accomplished your goals.

- Then do the checklist for that chapter in the Appendix.

- Finally, have a colleague do the same checklist.

Skills that apply to several phases

Although the 31 skills are assigned to one phase of the lesson, several can be applied to more than one phase. For example:

- *Yellow Light* – to both Teaching and Seatwork

- *Increasing Non-Verbal Signals* – all four phases

- *Overlap* – Teaching and Seatwork

- *Opposite Side of the Room* – Teaching and Seatwork

- *Verbal Rapport with the Hard to Reach* – Teaching and Seatwork

- *Walking Speed* – Teaching, Transition to Seatwork

- *Positive Reinforcement* – Teaching and Seatwork

- And virtually all of the third phase, Transition to Seatwork, could go under Seatwork.

Feedback

A teacher's classroom is a very private turf. Be appropriate when observing. Try to blend into the environment; keep the focus off yourself. Observing without giving feedback is excellent learning for the visitor. Sometimes we actually learn and see more than we do in our own room. It's like visiting another part of your world—we notice differences and when we return home, we actually can experience more vividly what is "common" practice. For teachers being observed, feedback is how they learn. Like a respectful world traveler, we want to see the classroom not from our own ethnocentric eyes but as an invited guest. These forms are designed to avoid judgements, evaluations, even praise. The colleague has asked for our presence with a specific emphasis in mind. STAY WITHIN THOSE PARAMETERS. It is recommended that the feedback be immediate. The very best way is for the teacher being observed to give the students seatwork and be unavailable to the pupils for five to ten minutes. Both the teacher and the observer stay in the classroom. An observation would look like this:

- five to fifteen minute observation

- five to ten minute feedback

Make sure that the scheduled time, length of both observation and feedback, appropriate forms and any other pertinent information are arranged and provided. If the feedback can't be done immediately, do it at the earliest opportunity. Do it privately—the faculty lunch table isn't always exclusive enough.

Ending the Feedback

The underlying purpose of any coaching is professional development. From Madeline Hunter through Bruce Joyce and Bev Showers to Robert Garmston and Arthur Costa, the key, as a coach, is how to have the observed teacher be empowered. Our goal as coaches is to assist the teacher in owning his or her progress; otherwise, we inadvertently enable dependent behavior.

As we finish the feedback, gently use questions which encourage the teacher to reflect in a detached, long term manner. For example:

"Where do you see yourself in terms of mastering this skill?"

"What would you do next to further cement this skill?"

"Where does this skill fit with other skills from the same phase of a lesson?" or

"How does this skill dovetail and reinforce previously learned skills?"

"What is your next focus of professional development? Specifically, how would you go about doing that?"

Legality

To respect the originality of the author's copyright, the following conditions exist: the purchaser of this book has full permission to copy and utilize any and all pages on him or herself. This includes:

- the "self forms" of Chapters One through Five;

- a peer who has not purchased ENVoY may fill out forms from Chapters Six through Ten on you;

- your filling out Chapters Six through Ten on a peer. This latter is intended for your practice as an observer and is not to be shared, in any way, with the teacher you observe.

- Teachers may read and study school-owned books; however, they are not permitted to duplicate the forms. Only teachers who own their own books may duplicate the forms.

Footnote: Watch for an opportunity to be exposed to and trained in Arthur Costa's and Robert Garmston's Cognitive Coaching. It is an excellent macro-model; ENVoY is a micro-model.

Chapter Six: The Seven Gems

"An ENVoY peer supports colleagues to professionally grow and lets them decide in which area."
ENVoY

Because the Seven Gems cover all four phases of a lesson, they are more important than all of the rest of the ENVoY skills. Therefore, encourage each other to be wise enough to master the Seven Gems before practicing the other skills. In many cases, the techniques of Chapter Seven through Ten are refinements of Chapter Six. READ AND DO THIS CHAPTER BEFORE ANY OTHERS.

Notes on the Seven Gems

Freeze Body—As with all of the skills, support the teacher as he explores doing the technique in the least recommended way and then the recommended way. This allows him to self-discover what works for him.

ABOVE (Pause) Whisper—Explore with the teacher when he would want to use the method of using his voice above the class' collective volume, pause and drop to a whisper or when he would want to do the step-down approach.

Raise Your Hand vs. Speak Out—Help the teacher identify and consistently use verbal skills and non-verbal gestures for the three modes of Teacher Alone, Raise Your Hand and Speak Out. The technique of being able to be sensitive to these modes is sophisticated and a conversation about the ramifications of each might be appropriate.

Exit Directions—Really encourage the teacher to laminate between six and thirty directions that are routinely used.

Most Important Twenty Seconds— Actually time the teacher's pause with the second hand on your watch. Most teachers feel uncomfortable pausing for that long of a time period. Reassure the teacher that the teacher's patience during the pause is beneficial to the students and seems much shorter to them.

OFF/Neutral/ON—Most of the ENVoY skills are group management skills. This and the next skill involve how the teacher interacts with individual students. Be respectful of the fact that the teacher knows the pupils' circumstances better than the coach.

Influence Approach—Make sure the teacher has competency in the *OFF/Neutral/ ON* skill before doing this technique.

Freeze Body

During a lesson, we often alternate between students doing seatwork and cooperative learning to paying attention to the teacher's direct instruction. During a given fifteen-minute time period, the instructor can ask the class to shift their focus of attention as many as three times.

Congruency

What happens when there is a discrepancy between the teacher's verbal message of STOP and the teacher's non-verbal communication of MOVE? As the teacher asks the students to STOP what they are doing, they will look up and, if the teacher is walking, they notice that he is non-verbally contradicting himself by continuing to MOVE. As a result, they tend to go back to what they were previously doing.

Least Recommended vs. Recommended

The teacher wants feedback on the differences of how the class becomes attentive when the teacher MOVES while asking for attention compared to freezing while asking. The teacher will arrange to have the pupils shift their focus between seatwork and cooperative learning to paying attention to the teacher at least three to four times during a ten to fifteen minute period. If the teacher is going to do only two shifts back towards the teacher, then only do 2A and 3A.

Teacher's name _____ Observer _____

Freeze Body

1. List of teacher's favorite saying(s) that indicate that the instructor wants the students' attention: _____

_____

_____

Least Recommended

2 A.   The teacher will intentionally be moving while verbally indicating to the students to STOP. Describe the class' reaction to the teacher's request: _____

_____

_____

2 B.   The teacher will again intentionally move while verbally indicating to the students to STOP. Describe the class' reaction to the teacher's request: _____

_____

_____

Recommended

3 A.   The teacher will non-verbally signal you that he will now switch and freeze while asking the students to STOP. Describe the class' reaction to the teacher's request: _____

_____

_____

3 B.   The teacher will again freeze while asking the students to STOP. Describe the class' reaction to the teacher's request: _____

_____

Describe the difference between what happens when the teacher verbally indicates STOP while non-verbally moving compared to the same request being made with a *Freeze Body*:

_____

_____

_____

Teacher's name _____ Observer _____

ABOVE (Pause) Whisper

There are a variety of ways to get a class' attention. The two recommendations that the teacher has been practicing are to P A U S E once the instructor has the students' attention and to lower his voice once he has P A U S E D.

The teacher wants feedback on how attentive the class becomes when the recommendations are done compared to when they are not done. The teacher will arrange the lesson so that during your ten-to fifteen-minute visit, the instructor will be requesting the class' attention at least three to four times. If the teacher is able to request the class' attention only twice during your stay, then the teacher will only do 2 A and 3 A.

Drop Voice

Date of observation _____

1. List of teacher's favorite saying(s) that indicate the instructor wants the students' attention: _____

_____

Least Recommended

2A. The teacher will intentionally *not pause* or lower his voice after requesting the class' attention in his favorite way. As the observer, you will describe the two or three sentences the teacher uses to request the class' attention (without pausing or lowering his voice). Describe the class' attentiveness:_____

_____

2B. The teacher will again intentionally *not pause* or lower his voice after requesting the class' attention in his favorite way. As the observer, you will describe the two or three sentences the teacher uses to request the class' attention (without pausing or lowering his voice). Describe the class' attentiveness:_____

_____

Recommended

3A. The teacher will non-verbally signal you that he will now switch and do the P A U S E after getting the students' attention and will drop to a lower whisper. The teacher will do this maneuver twice. Describe the class' attentiveness: _____

_____

_____

ABOVE (Pause) Whisper

Discuss with the teacher the difference between what happens when the teacher doesn't P A U S E and keeps his voice loud compared to when a P A U S E with a whisper is done.

Worst Day Scenario

The teacher has practiced the above skills for regular school days. The teacher has also practiced a modified technique that works well on right-brain days (e.g., the week before winter vacation, picture day, etc.). For these days, the teacher's call for attention has to be above the class' collective volume and has to be done quickly to shock or interrupt the class. At that point, the length of the P A U S E and what follows the P A U S E involves a sophisticated skill of timing. The teacher has a very short time span to lead the class into the content area. The teacher's two choices are:

The step-down, in some cases, is the instructor's only salvation, but it takes more discipline and control for the teacher to bring his voice volume all the way down through his normal range and then below. For both the drop and the step-down, it is recommended that the teacher elongate his sentences, slow his voice down and give it a softer timbre. This will put the class in a more listening mode.

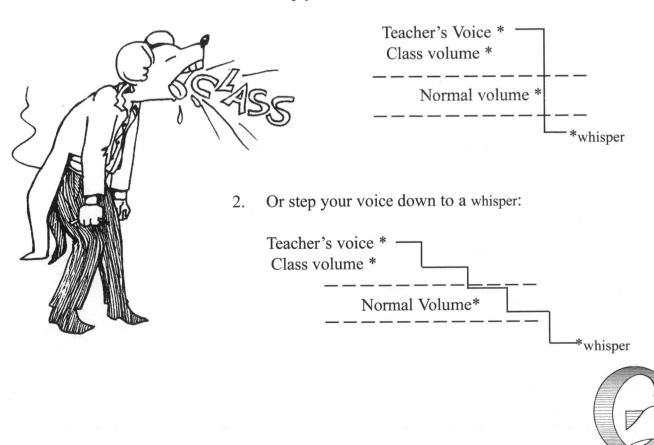

1. Drop your voice to a whisper:

2. Or step your voice down to a whisper:

Teacher's name _____ Observer _____

ABOVE (Pause) Whisper

Step Down Voice

1. The teacher has invited you to observe because he anticipates that the class will be louder than usual because it is a right-brain day.

Date of observation: _____

The teacher and the observer have identified the following conditions that make the day a right- brain day: _____

_____

_____

2. The teacher will attempt to do the drop maneuver mentioned above. If this technique isn't getting the class' attention, the teacher will switch to the step-down approach. You will do an observation as to which non-verbal communication the teacher did that was effective. Try to describe as specifically as possible how the teacher's behavior affected the class' attentiveness.

Description: _____

_____

_____

_____

_____

_____

_____

_____

Discuss with the teacher in the upcoming weeks when the right brain days might occur.

_____

_____

_____

_____

Raise Your Hand vs. Speak Out

During the Teaching portion of a lesson, the educator selects whether she wants to convey information to the class through lecture or have the class be interactive with the teacher. There are three formats for the teaching phase of a lesson and three ways the formats can be communicated to the students:

FORMATS:	Teacher Only One Talking	Raise Your Hand	Speak Out
LEVELS:			
Verbal:	"Listen up." "My turn."	"Raise your hand if..."	"Everyone."
Non-Verbal:	teacher pointing to self, hand in a traffic cop gesture of a "stop sign."	teacher models by raising her hand.	teacher gestures from class back toward self.

Momentum: (This occurs once the teacher has done the same format for several consecutive times.) The teacher will ask you to give her feedback on how she is implementing the formats on the different levels. Please familiarize yourself with the recommended strategies for implementing the formats and levels.

Safest Method

The safest method for a teacher to establish a format is to use both the verbal level and, at the same time, model with a gesture. Every time the teacher switches to a new mode, the teacher considers doing the verbal and non-verbal messages together.

Better Maneuver

The better maneuver is for the teacher to initially do both the verbal and non-verbal level together for at least two consecutive times, then drop the verbal level and do just the non-verbal signal. The non-verbal level has many by-products: the room is quieter, the students become more visual, the students are watching the teacher more, the teacher's voice is reserved for either content or positive reinforcement.

Ultimate Technique

The ultimate technique for the teacher is to progress from the verbal and non-verbal level through the non-verbal level alone to dropping the non-verbal signal and noticing that the class will still remain in the current operating mode most of the time.

Be Sensitive

The teacher especially wants to be sensitive when she switches from the Speak Out mode. She wants to drop her voice and hold still when she initiates the Teacher Only One Talking or Raise Your Hand. In other words, using the diagram at the top of this page, the teacher is OK when moving from columns in a left to right direction but needs to be cautious when going from the right to left.

Raise Your Hand vs. Speak Out

When the observer meets with the teacher before the observation, have the teacher share what her style is in terms of the verbal and non-verbal levels. Fill in this chart so you, the observer, can recognize these levels:

FORMATS:	Teacher Only One Talking	Raise Your Hand	Speak Out
Verbal:	_____	_____	_____
	_____	_____	_____
Non-Verbal:	_____	_____	_____
	_____	_____	_____
	_____	_____	_____

Already Doing

The observer will interview the teacher and learn which formats and levels the teacher has done for some time: _____

_____

_____

_____

Practicing New Habits

And which ones are new: _____

_____

_____

_____

By talking to the teacher, the observer will know which of the recommended strategies the teacher will be practicing and will want feedback on; therefore, all four recommended strategies are listed.

Teacher's name _____ Observer _____

Raise Your Hand vs. Speak Out

Strategies

Below are the four recommended strategies. Put a check for each time one of the recommended strategies was done. Also, describe the verbal and non-verbal communication that was employed.

The Safest Method:

The teacher employs both the verbal and non-verbal messages every time she initiates each of the modes.

Date of implementation: _____

Describe the results:

Teacher Only One Talking: _____

_____

Raise Your Hand: _____

_____

Speak Out: _____

_____

The Better Maneuver:

The teacher uses the verbal and non-verbal messages when she initiates a mode. Then after doing both the verbal and non-verbal messages two or three times, the teacher drops the verbal and does just the non-verbal message. Describe how long the verbal and non-verbal messages had to be used together before the teacher was able to drop the verbal and do just the non-verbal communication.

Teacher Only One Talking: _____

_____

Raise Your Hand: _____

_____

Speak Out: _____

_____

Teacher's name _____ Observer _____

Raise Your Hand vs. Speak Out

Strategies

The Ultimate Technique

The teacher does the verbal and non-verbal communications together, then drops the verbal level and then eventually drops the non-verbal messages. Describe how long the teacher had to do the non-verbal gesture alone before she could drop it and the class would still do the mode:

Teacher Only One Talking: _____

_____

Raise Your Hand: _____

_____

Speak Out: _____

_____

Be Sensitive When

The sequence that most educators report as the most dangerous is when the instructor switches from more to less student involvement. For the majority of teachers, the most volatile sequence is to move from Speak Out to Teacher Only One Talking. And progressively easier is from Speak Out to Raise Your Hand and Raise Your Hand to Teacher Only One Talking. When the instructor switches from more to less student involvement, the suggestion is that the teacher drops her voice and stands still. Record how the teacher handles these transitions. Report how the class responded. _____

_____

_____

_____

_____

_____

_____

_____

Exit Directions

When a teacher finishes the lecture or presentation portion of a lesson, a set of directions is usually given. These directions inform the class about assignments to be done either during seatwork or as homework or both. The directions mark the decrease in a teacher's availability and are labeled, *Exit Directions*. When *Exit Directions* are written on the board, there is a stable, visual representation of what was said.

Increasing Clarity

Visual *Exit Directions* both increase the clarity of the message and double the length of the memory. This, of course, frees the teacher from having to be a parrot repeating what was said. The instructor now can assist students one-on-one during the seatwork segment of the lesson.

The teacher has invited you in to give feedback on three aspects of the instructor's *exit directions*.

> ## *Watch for*
> 1. Thoroughness of information provided
> 2. Employing non-verbal signals
> 3. Use or potential use of lamination

Teacher's name _____ Observer _____

Exit Directions

1.   Comment on the thoroughness of the information provided, especially mentioning the when, where, what, in what form and what to do when finished. If students have questions, notice if the teacher refers back to the visual information on the board. By watching the students' reactions, you will know how clear and systematic the teacher is. _____

_____

_____

Employing Non-verbal Signals

2.   The best way for students to know which, of all the information on the board, are the *Exit Directions* is to be systematic in terms of where (location) and how (color of chalk used and writing style) they are listed. Some self-contained classroom teachers use different colors for different subjects, e.g., math is blue. Describe the non-verbal signals the teacher is using so that even a student who has been daydreaming and has returned to earth would know which, of all the information on the board, are the *Exit Directions*: _____

_____

_____

Lamination

3.   Teachers don't have time to fully write out the information stated in number one. A suggestion is to write out the information that is used on a regular basis on a tag board and then laminate the tag board. Sometimes the same information is used in the same manner over and over. Other times the teacher will want to leave blanks on the card where, using an erasable overhead transparency pen, the teacher can put the specific information for that particular day. If there is more than one content area involved, the teacher could use a separate card for each. Comment on the effectiveness of the information that is laminated and if any additional information could be laminated. _____

_____

_____

If the teacher so desires, an experiment could be done that would contrast the above recommended suggestions with the traditional "oral only" *Exit Directions*. If this is done, discuss with the teacher the length of time it took to finish the directions, number of times the same information is repeated, the general comfort or frustration level of the classroom and, finally, what happens when the daydreamers come back to earth and want to know, "What are we doing?"

Most Important Twenty Seconds

When the teacher finishes direct instruction and the students are about to begin their seatwork, a transition is being made from group-oriented to one-on-one help. This transition is best done through a combination of visual *Exit Directions* and by modeling expectations that they will be concentrating. The most productive seatwork atmosphere, whether it is the students working alone or with partners (e.g., cooperative learning), is a visual one...meaning purposeful, often silent but not necessarily so. Here are the suggestions on how to model this productive visual atmosphere.

Visual Atmosphere

1. The teacher reads the *Exit Directions*.

2. Teacher asks if there are any questions. If there are any questions, besides orally answering, the teacher writes the additional answers or information on the board.

3. Teacher releases the students with wording such as, "You may begin now."

4. *Most Important Twenty Seconds (MITS)*: teacher freezes his body and waits 20 seconds while the teacher models for the students how quiet and concentrating the teacher would like them to be. If students are requesting help by raising their hands or speaking out, the teacher keeps his eyes scanning the room, visually stays very still and, with hand gestures, indicates to those students that the teacher will be with them in a second. Some el-ementary teachers have a Hula Hoop[R] that they stand in during this *MITS*. The kinesthetic learners, who are seeking help, can see the physical hoop and are reminded in a concrete way that the teacher is not yet available.

5. The teacher slowly moves to help the students individually.

Least Recommended vs. Recommended

The teacher will arrange that the transition from direct instruction to independent seatwork is done during the five to ten minutes the observer is in the room. The teacher has a choice of doing either the recommended technique or the least recommended technique. If the observer is coming more than once, the teacher can do the least recommended technique on the first visit and the recommended technique on the second visit. By doing a contrast, the observer can give the teacher feedback on the effectiveness of the recommended technique.

Teacher's name _____ Observer _____

Most Important Twenty Seconds

Date of observation: _____

Yes/No   1. The teacher is doing the recommended approach.

Yes/No   2. The *Exit Directions* are done visually.

Yes/No   3. Teacher asked if there were any questions.

Yes/No   The teacher wrote any additional information on the board.

Yes/No   4. The teacher used a verbal signal to release the class.

Yes/No   5. *MITS (Most Important Twenty Seconds)* was done with body frozen and the teacher remained group-oriented (instead of individually-oriented) and signaled non-verbally that those students requesting assistance would be helped in a little while.

Yes/No   6. Then, the teacher slowly moved to help students individually.

Least Recommended

If the teacher selected the least recommended approach, discuss the insights of how the teacher's actions affected the students' response. _____

_____

_____

_____

_____

_____

Recommended

If the teacher selected the recommended approach, discuss the insights of how the teacher's actions affected the students' response. _____

_____

_____

_____

_____

_____

Teacher's name _____ Observer _____

OFF/Neutral/ON

The teacher has already practiced this *OFF/Neutral/ON* concept and filled out the corresponding self form.

Some students are often OFF task and when the teacher approaches them, they hold their breath until the teacher leaves, at which time, they tend to breathe and go OFF task again.

OFF/Neutral/OFF

We are going to identify these students as "OFF to Neutral to OFF" students. There are usually two to four students who fit this category. Since the teacher is learning this new process skill, he has not selected his worst case students. Instead, the teacher has selected some marginal students.

For a given seatwork time period, the teacher will intentionally approach these students in a rushed and punitive manner and you, the observer, will notice whether they tend to hold their breath. The teacher will only stay a short time and the observer will notice if the students tend to go OFF task after the teacher leaves.

Least Recommended Approach

Describe how long the teacher stayed, what the breathing pattern of the student was and how long after the teacher left did the student go OFF task.

First student's initials or description of: _____

Description of the teacher's approach and how long the teacher stayed: _____

_____

Description of the student's breathing pattern and when the student returned to OFF task: _____

Second student's initials or description of: _____

Description of the teacher's approach and how long the teacher stayed: _____

_____

Description of the student's breathing pattern and when the student returned to OFF task: _____

Third student's initials or description of: _____

Description of the teacher's approach and how long the teacher stayed: _____

_____

Description of the student's breathing pattern and when the student returned to OFF task: _____

Teacher's name _____ Observer _____

OFF/Neutral/ON

During this same seatwork time period, the teacher will approach them in a slow manner and stay until they finally breathe and go back ON task. IT IS IMPERATIVE THAT THE STUDENT IS ON TASK AND HAS BREATHED AT LEAST TWICE BEFORE THE TEACHER LEAVES. When the teacher slowly leaves, notice if the teacher moves away from the student's backside so that the student doesn't know when the instructor actually left. Observer will describe speed of approach, how long the teacher stayed until the student was breathing and on task, if the teacher moved away from the student's backside and how long the student stayed on task after the teacher left.

During the debrief, it is suggested that the teacher and observer share which other students may benefit from these techniques.

Recommended Approach

Describe how long the teacher stayed, what the breathing pattern of the student was and how long after the teacher left did the student go ON task.

First student's initials or description of: _____

Description of the teacher's approach and how long the teacher stayed: _____

_____

Description of the teacher's exiting and how long the student stayed ON task: _____

_____

Second student's initials or description of: _____

Description of the teacher's approach and how long the teacher stayed: _____

_____

Description of the teacher's exiting and how long the student stayed ON task: _____

_____

Third student's initials or description of: _____

Description of the teacher's approach and how long the teacher stayed: _____

_____

Description of the teacher's exiting and how long the student stayed ON task: _____

_____

Influence Approach

It is IMPERATIVE that both the teacher and the observer have completed the *OFF/Neutral/ON* skillsheets and the corresponding "self form" of this skillsheet before beginning this.

The teacher is practicing using *Influence* instead of power. The teacher who uses power conveys the feeling of being personally threatened by the student who is inappropriate and, consequently, the intervention is "confrontational." The instructor using *Influence* is separating the student as a person from the student's behavior. The focus is on getting the student back to work. Why is this so important? We have suggested that there is an increasing number of students who don't have a lot of human contact with adults at home. We know that a student's number one preference is to have positive contact but his second preference is to have any contact rather than no contact. This student is willing to get in trouble in order to have adult contact. A poet once said, "A child will get our attention; the question of whether it is positive or negative is based on how soon and often we give it." This section is designed to break the "negative reinforcement syndrome."

From a Distance

Our goal is to increase how far the teacher can be from the student and still be able to manage because the farther away the teacher is, the more the student tends to believe that he is ON task because of himself instead of the teacher's presence. This truly is *INFLUENCE*.

As the observer records the indirect interaction between the teacher and the two selected students, watch for the innuendoes of *Influence*. At the same time be sensitive to the teacher's perceptions. She knows the students better than the observer and may feel very good about the level of *Influence* she was able to achieve compared to normal.

Indirect Influence

1. Teacher moves toward the student without looking at the student (e.g., the teacher is at a 45 degree angle from the front of the student's face).

2. As soon as the student stops being OFF task, the teacher PAUSES.

3. The teacher is looking at an adjacent student's work while peripherally (indirectly) watching the off-task student. The teacher wants to see if the student goes from Neutral to ON task. Teacher waits until the student breathes because when the student breathes, he will tend not to stay Neutral but, hopefully, go ON task. If the student starts to go back OFF, the teacher will immediately move closer to the student.

4. Once the student is ON task and has breathed twice, then the teacher will go to the student's side. At this point the teacher has many choices: to talk or not, to make eye contact or just look at the work, etc. The choice is based on how to best change the above mentioned "negative reinforcement syndrome" into a "positive contact." Teachers use this axiom when experimenting.

Teacher's name _____ Observer _____

Influence Approach

Recommended

The teacher has selected two students with whom she wants to practice this technique. Remember that it is easier for a teacher to learn a new skill by practicing with a "marginal student" than the "worst case" student. It takes more *timing* with the latter group.

First Student

First student's initials or description of: _____

1.   The teacher approaches the first student indirectly. How far away from the student was the teacher able to be when the student switched from OFF to at least Neutral? _____

_____

_____

_____

2.   Describe what the teacher saw that indicated that the student was going from OFF to Neutral (if possible, mention his breathing pattern): _____

_____

_____

_____

3.   The teacher has waited until the student breathed. If he went from Neutral toward OFF, describe what the teacher did: _____

_____

_____

_____

4.   The student has been ON task and has breathed twice. Describe what choice the teacher made and how the goal of "positive contact" was increased: _____

_____

_____

_____

Teacher's name _____ Observer _____

Influence Approach

Recommended

Second Student

Second student's initials or description of: _____

1. The teacher approaches the second student indirectly. Describe how far away from the student was the teacher able to be when the student switched from OFF to at least Neutral:

_____

_____

_____

2. Describe what the teacher saw that indicated that the student was going from OFF to NEUTRAL (if possible, mention his breathing pattern): _____

_____

_____

_____

3. The teacher has waited until the student breathed. If he went from Neutral toward OFF, describe what the teacher did: _____

_____

_____

_____

4. The student has been ON task and has breathed twice. Describe what choice the teacher made and how the goal of "positive contact" was increased: _____

_____

_____

_____

Mouse Doodles

Be ambitious enough to be patient.
Practice one skill a week.

Roll-on deodorant was realized in 1955—seven years after it was first conceived. Nylon was first conceived in 1927. How many years before it was realized?

Chapter Seven: Getting Their Attention

"Execution is the chariot of genius."
William Blake

Notes on Specific Skills

Freeze Body Refinements—Each teacher will idiosyncratically determine which of the refinements apply to him. Accept whatever the teacher indicates is the case for him.

Opening Visual Instructions—This skill is an emergency skill; therefore, the coach has to have a lot of permission from the teacher in order to invite a peer in to observe him practicing this skill. Be gentle when providing feedback on this skill.

Incomplete Sentences—This is one of the easiest skills of ENVoY's thirty-one techniques. Encourage the teacher to use it whenever appropriate. Please note that *Break & Breathe* is mentioned.

Positive Comments—This skill is designed more for the elementary teacher. It isn't as generic as the other skills.

Decontaminating the Classroom—This skill has consistently been evaluated as ENVoY's most beneficial technique. It really deserves to be ranked among the Seven Gems. Encourage each other to perfect this skill. Remind the teacher that when *Decontaminating...* is used for discipline, it is only designed for group, not individual, discipline.

Break & Breathe—This is the author's favorite and ENVoY's number one stress management technique. Since the teacher cannot predictably "schedule" a disciplinary situation, the peer may want to notice when such a situation arises during an observation of another skill. However, you would give feedback only if the teacher broached the subject.

Yellow Light—Cooperative Learning is often utilized by the teacher as part of the **Teaching Phase** of the lesson. *Yellow Light* is extremely helpful in making the transition back to a focus on the teacher.

Gender Reminder

When applicable, the teacher is referred to with the male pronoun and the student with the female pronoun.

Freeze Body Refinements

The teacher is going to experiment to see which, if any, of these refinements to *Freeze Body* increase the speed and ease with which the class becomes attentive when requested to do so. These techniques are:

> ## Refinement Techniques
> * Being in front of the room
> * Toes pointed ahead
> * Weight on both feet
> * Brief directions

Right Brain Days

Because *Freeze Body* is such a powerful variable, these refinements may not make any difference. So why practice the refinements? There are two reasons: to find out if they do make a difference and, secondly, because on right-brain days (e.g., Homecoming, picture day, etc.), they augment *Freeze Body's* effectiveness.

Since these are refinement skills of *Freeze Body*, the teacher will hold his body still while doing them so that the refinement variable(s) can be isolated and their impact determined.

The teacher will arrange to ask for the students' attention at least three to four times during the observer's fifteen-minute visit. If the teacher is able to request the class' attention only twice during the observer's stay, then the teacher will do only 2A and 3A.

"CLASS, LOOK UP HERE."

Teacher's name _____ Observer _____

Freeze Body Refinements

1. The teacher will determine which of these four techniques he wants to experiment with: location, toes, weight or length. The teacher could choose all four at once or isolate them. The ones selected are: _____

_____

Least Recommended

2 A.   The teacher will intentionally do the opposite of the refinement skills mentioned in number 1. For example: The teacher will not be in front of the room, have his toes pointed to the side, have more weight on one leg (with maybe a hand on the hip) and use a long sentence when requesting the students' attention. Describe the effect on the speed and ease in which the class responds. _____

_____

2 B.   The teacher will again intentionally do the opposite of the refinement skills mentioned in number 1. Describe the effect on the speed and ease in which the class responds.

_____

_____

Recommended

3 A.   The teacher will non-verbally signal the observer that the instructor will now switch and do the recommended techniques listed in number 1. Describe the class' speed and ease when they responded to the request for attention. _____

_____

3 B.   The teacher will do the recommended techniques a second time. Describe the class' speed and ease when they responded to the request for attention. _____

_____

_____

Describe the difference between what happens when the teacher isn't in the front, weight more on one leg, toes pointed out and uses a long sentence compared to when the teacher is in the front with his weight on both legs, toes pointed ahead and uses a short phrase when asking for attention. _____

_____

_____

Opening Visual Instructions

If the board has the directions on what the students are to do when they enter the room, they can **see** what to do. This is important because it is not being delivered orally. Visual messages make for a quieter classroom, students have a higher self-esteem and the teacher's energy level is higher.

Academic Warm-up

There are several purposes for the visual instructions. Often teachers will put on the board an academic warm-up activity. Frequently this is a fun-oriented, pencil and paper activity covering previous content: e.g., a review problem for math; copying a new vocabulary term and its definition or high-interest trivia question. The activity has to be within the students' abilities so that they are independent of the teacher; otherwise, it would be "teaching" instead of a "warm-up to teaching."

Transition

Besides using the board for academic warm-up activities, another reason is to assist the transition to the first activity. For instance, "Have a pencil and paper out and open your history book to page 127."

Least Recommended vs. Recommended

Preparation: The teacher and the observer will meet ahead of time and indicate which kind of opening visual instruction will be used: "academic warm-up" or "transition" (fill out #1). Also indicate if the teacher is going to do non-verbal modeling of attentiveness toward the board or do it the less effective way (fill out #2). It is recommended that after doing #1 through 5 at least once, the teacher does the emergency, "When There is No Time," which starts at #6.

Teacher's name _____ Observer _____

Opening Visual Instructions

1. Check for which purpose the teacher is using opening visual instructions:

    ____ academic warm-up   ____ transition

2. Our goal is to have the students non-verbally go into the appropriate mental state. The teacher is going to do this by visual instructions. What is the teacher's style of accomplishing this? Does he have the instructions hidden under a pull-down map or on an overhead that is turned off, and only after he has greeted them, are the instructions revealed? Does he have the instructions shown as the class walks into the room and is he at the door greeting the pupils? Does he have the instructions shown as they enter and is he standing still at the front modeling attention to the board while greeting the pupils? Since the contention is that the teacher's non-verbal communication is the single most powerful factor in a classroom, the teacher's modeling of attentiveness to the board is essential. To test this, do the opposite: have the instructions on the board and be moving and doing non-relevant talking while the students enter.

Least Recommended vs. Recommended

Circle if the teacher plans to do:

____ the more effective modeling (doing the opening visual instructions the recommended way).

____ the movement and non-relevant talking (doing the opening visual instructions the opposite from the recommended way).

3. Description of the instructions on the board: _____

    _____

    _____

4. Description of either the teacher's modeling or movement and talking: _____

    _____

    _____

    _____

5. Description of the class' attentiveness and responsiveness to the instructions on the board: _____

    _____

    _____

Teacher's name _____ Observer _____

Opening Visual Instructions

Sometimes the teacher doesn't have the opportunity to prepare the directions visually ahead of time. The teacher has three options:

• Get the class' attention and then write the directions.

• Get the class' attention and then orally give the directions.

• Write the directions and then get the class' attention.

The second option will work on certain days and is faster than the third alternative although the third choice is the safest and most critical for right-brain days.

When There is No Time

6. The teacher will pretend he is preoccupied and not ready to start the class on time.

A. What was the teacher doing while pretending to be "preoccupied?" _____

_____

_____

B. Describe the teacher's pretended tension/urge to quiet the class: _____

_____

_____

C. What were the instructions that the teacher wrote on the board? Mention if laminated signs were used: _____

_____

_____

D. How did the teacher get the class' attention? Especially comment on whether the teacher stood still, whether he initially had a volume that was just above the students' collective loudness and whether he paused as they quieted: _____

_____

_____

E. Final comments on the effectiveness: _____

_____

_____

Teacher's name _____ Observer _____

Incomplete Sentences

Often teachers' training courses encourage the instructor to have everyone's attention before beginning, yet we know that when we use our voice for the pace of the lesson and our non-verbal signals for management, the students get into the lesson sooner and remember the lesson as content-oriented. So what are some non-verbal alternatives to getting the students' attention?

If the content is of high interest, the teacher can start the lesson and the students will respond; however, if the teacher suspects the interest will not be high enough, he can use *Incomplete Sentences*. Students who are not watching the teacher, but hear an abrupt stoppage in the middle of the initial phrase of the sentence, will tend to freeze and look up. This maneuver allows quick transition to attentiveness. Some examples are, "AS WE," "LOOKING AT," "NOTICE HOW THE." As the inattentive students engage the teacher, he repeats the sentence in its entirety and continues. Using the skills learned in *Above (Pause) Whisper*, the teacher says the *Incomplete Sentence* above their collective volume and then repeats the sentence in its entirety in a whisper. Incomplete sentences are often effective for those "straggler" students who are slower than other pupils to give the instructor their attention.

Incomplete Sentences can be used any time. The ideal time to employ this technique is on right-brain days (e.g., picture day, first snowfall, etc.) because the teacher wants to decrease authority and increase rapport. It is best to practice the timing this technique requires before the right-brain days arrive.

List two of the teacher's favorite introductory sentences.

_____

_____

The teacher will check one of the following two choices:

_____ This is a left-brain day and I am practicing the timing of this technique. Observer skip numbers 1D and 2D.

_____ This is a right-brain day and I am employing this previously practiced technique. Observer, pay particular attention to how the teacher moves his body and breathes as he finishes his incomplete phrase and the short silence that follows the incomplete phrase. Then the teacher will settle his body before saying the sentence in its entirety in a low whisper. Numbers 1D and 2D are where you will provide the teacher feedback on this *Break & Breathe* skill.

Teacher's name _____ Observer _____

Incomplete Sentences

First Example

1A. Time of first *Incomplete Sentence*: _____

1B. List incomplete phrase: _____

1C. Description of the teacher's voice volume during incomplete phrase, how still the teacher's body was during the phrase and the brief silence that followed: _____

_____

1D. Description of how the teacher breathed and moved his body after he had said the *Incomplete Sentence*: _____

_____

1E. Description of the teacher's lower voice volume and slower voice speed as the sentence was said in its entirety in a low whisper: _____

_____

1F. Describe the effect on the class' attentiveness, especially the stragglers: _____

_____

Second Example

2A. Time of second *Incomplete Sentence*: _____

2B. List incomplete phrase: _____

2C. Description of the teacher's voice volume during incomplete phrase, how still the teacher's body was during the phrase and the brief silence that followed: _____

_____

2D. Description of how the teacher moved his body and breathed as he said the *Incomplete Sentence*: _____

_____

2E. Description of the teacher's lower voice volume and slower voice speed as the sentence was said in its entirety in a low whisper: _____

_____

2F. Describe the effect on the class' attentiveness, especially the stragglers: _____

_____

Teacher's name _____ Observer _____

Positive Comments

Students through fourth grade love to be told by their teacher that they are doing well. When the teacher compliments a child who is doing something well during a transition time, that student can then serve as a role model for the others. Sometimes the teacher has to give the compliments to students adjacent to the inappropriate students so that the latter is aware of the former, e.g., "I like that Kelly is ready."

Fifth Grade and Beyond

Teachers need to be more careful when giving positive comments to older students. Teachers need to be more subtle in their positive comments. The kind of comments the teacher makes depends on the level of rapport with a class. If the teacher doesn't have as much rapport, then it's less appropriate to use the word "I" and better to offer collective praise as opposed to individual or small group praise.

The teacher wants feedback on his use of positive comments made during this transition time. While this skill is under the Getting Their Attention phase of the lesson, it is applicable under any phase of a lesson when there is a transition. The teacher will arrange to have three or more transitions during your fifteen-minute stay.

Grade level of class observed: _____

Circle which phase of the lesson you will be observing: Getting Their Attention, Teaching, Transition to Seatwork and Seatwork.

First Example

1A. Describe what the teacher said when he first used positive comments: _____

_____

1B. Which student or students were inappropriate and the teacher wanted to provide them with a model of appropriateness by using the positive comment maneuver? _____

_____

1C. How close were the student or students who received the positive comments to those who were inappropriate? _____

_____

1D. Description of the effect of the modeling of appropriateness on those who were inappropriate: _____

_____

Teacher's name _____ Observer _____

Positive Comments

Second Example

2A. Describe what the teacher said when he used positive comments the second time:

_____

2B. Which student or students were inappropriate and the teacher wanted to provide them with a model of appropriateness by using the positive comment maneuver? _____

_____

2C. How close were the student or students who received the positive comments to those who were inappropriate? _____

_____

2D. Description of the effect of the modeling of appropriateness on those who were inappropriate: _____

_____

Third Example

3A. Describe what the teacher said when he used positive comments the third time:

_____

3B. Which student or students were inappropriate and the teacher wanted to provide them with a model of appropriateness by using the positive comment maneuver? _____

_____

3C. How close were the student or students who received the positive comments to those who were inappropriate? _____

_____

3D. Description of the effect of the modeling of appropriateness on those who were

inappropriate: _____

_____

Any further insights or comments you can offer to the teacher? _____

_____

_____

Teacher's name _____ Observer _____

Decontaminating the Classroom

A teacher is involved in a wide variety of activities in a single day. When the instructor consistently does only one particular activity (e.g., group discipline) from one particular location, the students connect that spot with that activity. Because the educator has established the connection between the activity and that area of the room, the students tend to respond more quickly and more appropriately because they know what to expect. This connection applies not only to location but in all non-verbal communication. For instance, if the teacher consistently turns the overhead on when he wants the class to take notes, the pupils are signaled by the sound of the click of the switch, the noise of the fan and the brightness from the screen area.

By knowing what activities the teacher does in a week, the teacher can select which activities he wants to connect with a given location, face, voice, body posture and perhaps a prop. These will range from taking roll, abstract processing, class discussions, listening circle to one-on-one counseling and group discipline; decontaminating fits in all four phases of a lesson. It is placed here because the single most important activity to have a definite location for is "group discipline."

Systematic Connection

Since the teacher doesn't know when he will be doing group discipline, the observer will be giving feedback on any two or three activities where the teacher makes a systematic connection between some non-verbal representations and the activities. The non-verbal signals can be composed, in part, by location, voice, face, body posture, gesture and props. The teacher will arrange to do two or three activities during the observer's fifteen-minute stay. The teacher can decide if the observer will be watching the initial connection of the non-verbal signals to the activity or concept or if the observer is seeing a connection that has previously been established.

Before the observation, the teacher will fill out the A sections of each of the activities. During the observation, the observer will fill in B - D sections.

First Example

1A. Activity or concept: _____

Description of non-verbal message(s) connected to activity or concept: _____

_____

Will the observer be seeing an initial connection or an established connection? _____

_____

1B. Describe the actual non-verbal signals utilized: _____

Teacher's name _____ Observer _____

Decontaminating the Classroom

1C. What was the class' response to the connection? _____

_____

1D. Discuss the effectiveness of the connection.

Second Example

2A. Activity or concept: _____

Description of non-verbal message(s) connected to activity or concept: _____

_____

Will the observer be seeing an initial connection or an established connection? _____

_____

2B. Describe the actual non-verbal signals utilized: _____

_____

2C. What was the class' response to the connection? _____

_____

2D. Discuss the effectiveness of the connection.

Third Example

3A. Activity or concept: _____

Description of non-verbal message(s) connected to activity or concept: _____

_____

Will the observer be seeing an initial connection or an established connection? _____

_____

3B. Describe the actual non-verbal signals utilized: _____

_____

3C. What was the class' response to the connection? _____

_____

3D. Discuss the effectiveness of the connection.

Break & Breathe

Every mental state is both represented and maintained by an equivalent physical state. The relationship between the mind-body is so interconnected that a change in one state will be reflected in the other.

If the mental state one is in is not desired or appropriate, then shifting the body assists the change in the mental state. To greatly assist the shift in the emotional and mental state, simultaneously move the body (Break) while Breathing. This allows a greater separation from the previous state. The sooner the person recognizes the inappropriateness of the current state, the easier it is to break the state.

Application

This is why doing *Break & Breathe* at the end of group discipline (see *Decontaminating the Classroom)* allows the teacher and pupils to return to content and have amnesia regarding the group discipline that occurred. The other occasion that *Break & Breathe* is effective is when the teacher needs to raise his voice to get the class' attention (see *ABOVE (Pause) Whisper)*. In both the group discipline and using a loud voice to get the students' attention, the *Break & Breathe* maneuver separates the teacher's persona of a martinet from the teacher's persona as a kind, loving teacher.

Stress Management

Because the *Break & Breathe* is ENVoY's single most important stress management technique, we recommend that the teacher have the observer fill out this form on the following occasions:

- Group discipline (*Decontaminating the Classroom*)

- Individual discipline

- A loud *ABOVE (Pause) Whisper*

- *Incomplete Sentence* on a right-brain day

- An emergency situation where the teacher needs to shout

It is difficult to accurately predict when the classroom circumstance warrants the teacher raising his voice. Therefore, we recommend that the teacher give this skillsheet to the observer on days that the teacher estimates that an increase in management is likely. These are usually right-brain days. These days might see an increase of the first four occasions listed above. The fifth occasion (Emergency Shout) might be filled out if an observer happens to witness an occasion where the teacher has to shout in an emergency. If an emergency occurs, the observer could use the Emergency Shout session of this skillsheet in addition to the feedback on the designated skill.

Teacher's name _____ Observer _____

Break & Breathe

Group Discipline

The most important time to do the *Break & Breathe* is when the teacher has done group (see *Decontaminating the Classroom)* or individual discipline. Since we don't know when the teacher might be doing such an activity, he should schedule the observer to come in when he knows the pupils will be louder than normal. Any right-brain day would certainly qualify.

Date of Observation: _____

1. Describe a situation where it was appropriate for the teacher to do group discipline:

_____

_____

2. Describe how the teacher did *Break & Breathe*: _____

_____

3. Describe the beneficial results both for the teacher and the pupils: _____

_____

_____

Individual Discipline

Sometimes a teacher is working with student X and has to put student Y, who is across the room, back on task. The teacher knows it is better to use a minimal verbal message both for Y's self-esteem and so as not to disturb the other students who are on task (see *Maintaining the Productive Atmosphere: Mini MITS*). On this occasion, the teacher needs to raise his voice and verbally reprimand Y. If, when the teacher refocuses his attention back to X, he still may have residue left from having corrected Y, then X may unduly receive emotional debris. Therefore, the teacher, when finishing with Y, wants to stand straight up (and do a half step to the side) and breathe fully. The bigger the state that the teacher wants to get out of, the more important it is for him to breathe deeply twice.

1. Describe a situation where the teacher did individual discipline: _____

_____

_____

2. Describe how the teacher did *Break & Breathe:* _____

_____

Teacher's name _____ Observer _____

Break & Breathe

3. Describe the beneficial results both for the teacher, the student disciplined (Y), the student being academically helped (X) and the other pupils: _____

_____

_____

_____

A Loud ABOVE (Pause) Whisper

Date of observation: _____

1. Sometimes the collective volume in the room is loud and therefore the teacher has to do a loud, "Class". The teacher is susceptible to becoming frustrated as he strains his vocal chords. Describe a situation where the teacher did a loud "Class!" (*ABOVE*) in order to get their attention. _____

_____

_____

_____

2. Describe how the teacher did *Break & Breathe*: _____

_____

_____

3. Describe the beneficial results both for the teacher and the other(s) involved: _____

_____

_____

_____

Teacher's name _____ Observer _____

Break & Breathe

Severe Incomplete Sentence

Date of observation _____

1. As in the above example, there are times when the gentle approach to getting their attention isn't sufficient. Sometimes the teacher has to do a sharp *Incomplete Sentence* with a harsh expression on his face. The teacher is usually holding his breath high and shallow. Describe a situation when the teacher did a severe *Incomplete Sentence*. _____

_____

_____

2. Describe how the teacher did *Break & Breathe:* _____

_____

_____

3. Describe the beneficial results both for the teacher and the other(s) involved: _____

_____

_____

Emergency Shout

Date of observation _____

1. There are occasions when the teacher needs to yell or talk loudly because of an emergency situation. For example, a box of books is about to fall on some students and the teacher screams loudly, "Watch out!" The teacher needs to have both himself and his students recover from the adrenaline that was released inside their bodies. Describe an emergency situation when the teacher raised his voice: _____

_____

_____

2. Describe how the teacher did *Break & Breathe:* _____

_____

3. Describe the beneficial results both for the teacher and the other(s) involved: _____

_____

_____

Teacher's name _____ Observer _____

Yellow Light

There are a variety of situations when we need to get the class' attention. Sometimes it is the initial contact, like at the start of the class or during a structured group activity. It is respectful to signal them that the time is approaching to direct their attention back to the teacher. By doing the signaling before the actual time for direct instruction, the students can ready themselves. For example, "One minute to go." This is especially true when they are working in small groups. Think about what it would be like if we only had red and green lights at intersections; hence, this early warning signal will be labeled *Yellow Light*.

The teacher wants to experiment to see if the *Yellow Light* produces a smooth transition from the students being independent or peer-oriented to becoming teacher-oriented. The teacher will arrange a lesson that has the pupils alternate between doing activities at their desks and focusing back on the instructor. It would be especially beneficial if the desk activity was a cooperative learning activity. The teacher will arrange to have the class refocus back on the teacher at least four times during the observer's fifteen-minute stay. If the teacher is only able to arrange two refocuses back to the instructor, then the teacher will do only 1's.

Date of observation: _____

What was the lesson on? _____

Least Recommended

1. Teacher will have students doing a desk activity and intentionally, without a yellow light, ask them for their attention. Describe the speed and willingness of the students to focus on the teacher: _____

_____

_____

2. Teacher will have students doing a desk activity and again, intentionally, without a yellow light, ask them for their attention. Describe the speed and willingness of the students to focus on the teacher: _____

_____

_____

Teacher's name _____ Observer _____

Yellow Light

Recommended

1. The teacher will non-verbally signal the observer that the instructor will now switch to the recommended transition skill of yellow light. As the observer, pay attention to the teacher's volume when the yellow light is announced. The teacher wants the class to be aware of the announcement without distracting the pupils from the focus of the activity they are engaged in. Describe the volume and the class' ability to focus on the activity: _____

_____

Describe the speed and willingness of the students to focus on the teacher._____

_____

2. The teacher will again do the recommended transition skill of yellow light. As the observer, pay attention to the teacher's volume when the yellow light is announced and whether the students are able to continue the activity they are engaged in. Describe the volume and the class' ability to focus on the activity:_____

_____

Describe the speed and willingness of the students to focus on the teacher._____

_____

Transition to Teacher Only One Talking

The other occasion to use the yellow light is during the teacher's presentation when he wants to switch from the interaction of "students and teacher" back to "teacher alone." A typical announcement is, "OK, I will call on Janet and Frank and then we will..." Often, the teacher wants to make the announcement in a voice that is different from the voice he uses during presentations. You could even say that the teacher is using his voice like the commas in a sentence; his voice is parenthetical to the rest of the sentence.

1. What did the teacher say? _____

_____

2. Describe the teacher's voice volume: _____

_____

_____

3. Discuss if the *Yellow Light* made for a smoother transition as the class switched from the interactive activity back to a focus on the teacher.

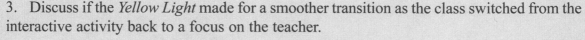

Chapter Eight: Teaching

*"We cannot not do non-verbal communication; the
only question is whether we are doing it systematically."*

Notes on Specific Skills:

Raise Your Hand vs. Speak Out

The instructions describing this skill are long. Feel free to simplify how to record the teacher's implementation of this technique.

Increasing Non-verbal Signals

This skill can be used in all four phases of a lesson. It can be applied to both the academic and the management arenas.

Overlap

This is one of the least frequently used skills that is easy to use. Help the teacher clarify when to use this technique. Sometimes the kinesthetic students need an opportunity to wiggle and move and overlap precludes this.

Opposite Side of the Room

This is a perennial favorite of teachers. This skill is very similar to the *Mini MITS* in that the teacher keeps the needs of the group in mind when the teacher interacts with an individual student.

Verbal Rapport With Hard to Reach Students

This is one of the few one-on-one skills that ENVoY includes. It is ideal for the At-Risk population. Because of the sophistication of this maneuver, more than one observation is recommended.

Use Action Words Last

Encourage the teacher to use the hand gesture. The palm down or toward the class is the same maneuver found in the Teacher Alone *Raise Your Hand vs. Speak Out.*

Gender Reminder

When applicable, the teacher is referred to with the female pronoun and the student with the male pronoun.

Teacher's name _____ Observer _____

Raise Your Hand vs. Speak Out Refinements

During the Teaching portion of a lesson when the teacher wants to be interactive with the class, there are two formats the instructor can utilize, Raise Your Hand or Speak Out. There are other variations of these two formats such as calling on one student or doing a Raise Your Hand, and then having the students Speak Out the answer in unison.

This skillsheet will test the following: If the interest in the content question is high, announce the format before you ask the content question; and if the interest in the content is low, ask the content question and then decide which format to announce.

The teacher wants feedback on how following or not following these axioms affects the class. The teacher will arrange to have you come for one longer visit (e.g., fifteen to twenty minutes) or two shorter visits (e.g., ten to fifteen minutes).

Recommended

High Interest Content

The teacher will non-verbally signal the observer that a high interest content question is about to be asked. For example, the teacher could show a "thumbs up" to indicate the content question will be of high interest. The teacher will do the recommended approach by first announcing the format, then asking the content question.

1. As an observer, verify that the class has high interest in the content: _____

    Circle the format that the teacher announced prior to the content question: Raise Your Hand, call on an individual student, Speak Out, Raise Your Hand then Speak Out the answer in unison or _____

    Describe results: _____

2. The teacher will again do the recommended approach. As an observer, verify that the class has high interest in the content: _____

    Circle the format that the teacher announced prior to the content question: Raise Your Hand, call on an individual student, Speak Out, Raise Your Hand then Speak Out the answer in unison or _____

    Describe results: _____

    _____

    _____

    _____

Teacher's name _____ Observer _____

Raise Your Hand vs. Speak Out Refinements

Recommended

Low Interest Content

The teacher will non-verbally signal the observer that a low interest content question is about to be asked. For example, the teacher could show a "thumbs down" to indicate this. The teacher will do the recommended approach by first asking the content question and then announcing what the format will be.

1. As an observer, verify that the class has low interest in the content question.

    _____

    _____

    How long did the teacher wait after she asked the content question and before she announced the format? _____

    Circle the format that was announced after the teacher said the content question: Raise Your Hand, call on an individual student, Speak Out, Raise Your Hand then Speak Out the answer in unison or _____

    Describe the results: _____

    _____

    _____

2. The teacher will again do the recommended approach. As an observer, verify that the class has little interest in the content question. _____

    _____

    _____

    How long did the teacher wait after she asked the content question and before she announced the format? _____

    Circle the format that was announced after the teacher asked the content question: Raise Your Hand, call on an individual student, Speak Out, Raise Your Hand then Speak Out the answer in unison or _____

    Describe the results: _____

    _____

    _____

Teacher's name _____ Observer _____

Raise Your Hand vs. Speak Out Refinements

The teacher has systematically done the formula of "interest high—format first" and "interest low—content question first." To test the validity of these recommendations, the teacher will do the opposite.

The teacher will non-verbally signal the observer that a high interest content question is about to be asked. For example, the teacher could show a "thumbs up" to indicate the content question will be of high interest. The teacher will also non-verbally signal that she will do the reverse of the recommended approach by saying the content question first. The signal might be the teacher turning the "thumbs up" gesture upside down.

Least Recommended

High Interest Content

1. As an observer, verify that the class has high interest in the content question:

_____

_____

How long did the teacher wait after she asked the content question and before she announced the format? _____

Circle the format that was announced after the teacher said the content question: Raise Your Hand, call on an individual student, Speak Out, Raise Your Hand then Speak Out the answer in unison or _____

Describe the results: _____

_____

2. The teacher will again do the opposite of the recommended approach. As an observer, verify that the class has high interest in the content question: _____

_____

_____

How long did the teacher wait after she asked the content question and before she announced the format? _____

Circle the format that was announced after the teacher said the content question: Raise Your Hand, call on an individual student, Speak Out, Raise Your Hand then Speak Out the answer in unison or _____

Describe the results: _____

_____

Teacher's name _____ Observer _____

Raise Your Hand vs. Speak Out Refinements

The teacher will non-verbally signal the observer that a low interest content question is about to be asked. For example, the teacher could show a "thumbs down" to indicate the content question will be of low interest. The teacher will also non-verbally signal that she will do the reverse of the recommended approach by saying the format first. The signal might be the teacher turning the "thumbs down gesture" right side up.

Least Recommended

Low Interest Content

1. As an observer, verify that the class has a low interest in the content question: _____

_____

_____

Circle the format that was announced before the teacher asked the content question: Raise Your Hand, call on an individual student, Speak Out, Raise Your Hand then Speak Out the answer in unison or _____

Describe the results: _____

_____

_____

2. The teacher will again do the opposite of the recommended approach. As an observer, verify that the class has a low interest in the content question: _____

_____

Circle the format that was announced before the teacher asked the content question: Raise Your Hand, call on an individual student, Speak Out, Raise Your Hand then Speak Out the answer in unison or _____

Describe the results: _____

_____

What conclusions can the teacher and you draw in comparing students' interest in the content with how the teacher asks the question? _____

_____

_____

Increasing Non-verbal Signals

Covering more content in a "win-win" atmosphere is one of the biggest benefits of being systematic with non-verbal signals. HOW? By using non-verbal signals for management, the teacher's voice can be used for the "pace of the lesson." In addition, academic non-verbal signals are preventive because they force the class to watch the instructor. This has the by-product of a quieter room and, with the students' eyes on the teacher, all the management non-verbal signals are available for the instructor to use.

The teacher meets with the observer and provides the following list of non-verbal signals that the teacher is trying to increase.

Non-verbal Signals		Usage/Meaning
a. _____	=	_____
_____	=	_____
b. _____	=	_____
_____	=	_____
c. _____	=	_____
_____	=	_____
d. _____	=	_____
_____	=	_____

The observer will especially watch for the above. However, there may be more non-verbal signals than those listed above; therefore, additional space is provided. During the Teaching phase of a lesson, the teacher will arrange to use several academic and management non-verbal signals that the observer will watch during a fifteen-minute stay.

Systematic Non-verbal Signals

Date of Observation: _____

Non-verbal Signals		Usage/Meaning
a. _____	=	_____
_____	=	_____
b. _____	=	_____
_____	=	_____

Teacher's name _____ Observer _____

Increasing Non-verbal Signals

Non-verbal Signals		Usage/Meaning
c. _____	=	_____
_____	=	_____
d. _____	=	_____
_____	=	_____
e. _____	=	_____
_____	=	_____
f. _____	=	_____
_____	=	_____
g. _____	=	_____
_____	=	_____

Since the teacher is literally trying to use her non-verbal signals for the format and her verbal level for the content, list those occasions when a verbal signal was used when it might have been more effective to either use a non-verbal signal alone or in conjunction with the verbal message.

Becoming Systematic

Verbal Messages		Suggested Non-verbal Signals
a. _____	=	_____
_____	=	_____
b. _____	=	_____
_____	=	_____
c. _____	=	_____
_____	=	_____
d. _____	=	_____
_____	=	_____

Share with the teacher your suggestions.

Teacher's name _____ Observer _____

Overlap

The more effective the teacher is, the more the teacher saves time and increases productivity. The teacher prepares the class with materials and instructions for the next activity while the class is still in the first activity. She is providing a smoother, quicker and easier transition to the next activity. The teacher will arrange to do an *Overlap* transition during the observer's ten-minute stay.

Kinesthetic Class

If it is a highly kinesthetic class, the teacher may want to have a break between one activity and another so that the students can get up, move around and release some energy. These are the times when it would be best not to use the *Overlap* technique.

1. Description of first activity being done: _____
_____
_____

2. Describe how the second activity was introduced while the first activity was still going on; mention if directions for the forthcoming activity were visually presented. Could some or all of the directions be laminated? _____
_____
_____
_____

3. Describe the transition from the end of the first activity and the flow into the second activity. _____
_____
_____
_____

4. Insights and comments from doing this observation: _____
_____
_____
_____

Teacher's name _____ Observer _____

Opposite Side of the Room

The traditional style of rapport is to move toward the person you are interacting with. While this is fine in a one-on-one situation, this habit of moving toward an individual does not work as well in the group setting of a classroom. The teacher has practiced doing a technique of trying to respectfully move to the opposite side of the room before calling on a student. The physical presence of the teacher will be a preventive management maneuver for those students close to the teacher while the teacher will be able to look across the room and non-verbally manage from afar. As an observer, notice the levels of class attentiveness when the teacher does the more traditional reaction of moving toward the student and when the teacher positions herself away from the student she calls on.

Least Recommended

The teacher will be in front of the class and call upon several students. Each time the teacher will intentionally move toward the student. It would be helpful if the teacher actually has her back to a portion of the class as she steps toward the student she called upon. This section of pupils intuitively knows that the teacher cannot see them. If this section is not as attentive as the pupils near the teacher's front, it may not be because they are intentionally being impolite. They may be interpreting the teacher's behavior as indicating that the instructor's interaction does not involve them. Observe which portions of the room have high, average and low levels of attentiveness.

1st time _____

_____

2nd time _____

_____

Recommended

As prearranged, the teacher signals that she will be switching to the "Opposite Side of the Room" technique. Record the effect this maneuver has on the class' attentiveness.

Your observations:

1st time _____

_____

2nd time _____

_____

Teacher's name _____ Observer _____

Verbal Rapport With Hard to Reach Students

There is a certain percentage of students who are not motivated by the teacher's credentials or authority. These students can be reached through rapport. One form of rapport is to include in the teacher's lesson something that is of high interest to them.

They become much more attentive when they're interested. The teacher would like feedback from you, the observer, on how she is implementing some techniques that she has been practicing with these *Hard to Reach Students*. The teacher will fill out all 1's and 2's.

Hard to Reach Students

1. **First student's** initials or description of who fits the five to fifteen percent of the student population who is *Hard to Reach*. These students are usually right-brain oriented and are more or less not affected by standard disciplinary systems. _____

2. List the two or three items of high interest for this student: _____
_____
_____

3. While the teacher is presenting or working one-on-one with this pupil, the instructor will spice up the content of the lesson with the student's high-interest items. The teacher will attempt to do this twice. Observer lists the example(s) and describes the change in the student's attentiveness: _____
_____
_____

1. **Second student's** initials or description of who is *Hard to Reach*: _____

2. List the two or three items of high interest for this student: _____
_____
_____

3. While the teacher is presenting or working one-on-one with this pupil, the instructor will spice up the content of the lesson with the student's high-interest items. The teacher will attempt to do this twice. The observer lists the example(s) and describes the change in the student's attentiveness. The teacher can do the first and second student during the same lesson: _____
_____
_____

Teacher's name _____ Observer _____

Verbal Rapport With Hard to Reach Students
Adolescents and Above

When teaching students in the lower grades, the teacher can look at the student as the instructor talks about the Hard to Reach student's high-interest areas. When teaching adolescents and above, it is more effective not to look at the student as the instructor sprinkles in parts of the high-interest areas. If the teacher looks at the pupil while saying these high-interest areas, the student knows the teacher is doing this intentionally. But if the teacher is beginning to say the student's high-interest item and partially turns away from the student as the student begins to look at the teacher, the student doesn't know for sure what the teacher's purpose was. The student is drawn to the teacher and that intrigues the pupil; right-brain oriented people love to be intrigued. Behaviorally, the student's eyes are following the teacher as the teacher turns away from the student. The student is chasing, choosing, selecting the instructor. The teacher will fill out all 1's and 2's before observation.

Adolescents and Above

1. **First person's** initials or description of: _____

2. List the person's two or three areas of high interest: _____

_____

3. While the teacher is lecturing and the targeted student is not attentive, the teacher will mention the items of high interest. As an observer, describe if the instructor partially turned away from the student as the pupil began to look toward the teacher. Also, describe the change in the student's attentiveness: _____

_____

1. **Second person's** initials or description of: _____

2. List the person's two or three areas of high interest: _____

_____

_____

3. While the teacher is lecturing and the targeted student is not attentive, the teacher will mention the items of high interest. As an observer, describe if the instructor partially turned away from the student as the pupil began to look toward the teacher. Also, describe the change in the student's attentiveness: _____

_____

Teacher's name _____ Observer _____

Verbal Rapport With Hard to Reach Students
Timing

The longer a student is inattentive, the stronger the student's daydream becomes. Therefore, as soon as the teacher sees a student start to fade from attentiveness, the instructor will want to mention the student's areas of high interest so that the student is more likely to hear the comments. The teacher will do the least recommended way initially and then the recommended way of mentioning the high-interest item as soon as the student begins to drift off. If the teacher is unable to do 3 - 6 during the same lesson, then the instructor will do 3 & 5 during this lesson and 4 & 6 during another lesson.

Timing

1. Initials of a right-brain oriented student or description of: _____

2. The person's two or three areas of high interest: _____

Least Recommended

3. While the teacher is lecturing and when the student has faded off into something other than what the instructor is covering, the teacher will spice up the content with areas of high interest to the student. As an observer, describe the teacher's voice volume and any changes in the student's attentiveness: _____

4. The teacher will do this maneuver again with the same student. It would be best if the instructor did a repeat of this technique during the same lecture. As the observer, describe the teacher's voice volume and any changes in the student's attentiveness: _____

_____

Recommended

5. The teacher will switch and sprinkle the interest items into the presentation just as the student begins to drift off. The teacher will do this during the same lesson that 3 was done. As much as possible, the teacher will keep her voice volume the same as 3. As observer, describe the teacher's voice volume and the degree that the student becomes attentive.

_____

6. The teacher will do the recommended approach of 5 again. The instructor will do this during the same lesson as 4. The teacher will try to keep her voice volume the same as 3. As the observer, describe the teacher's voice volume and the degree that the student becomes attentive: _____

As an observer, what insights can you offer the teacher in terms of the effectiveness of the recommended approach? Discuss how powerful it is if the teacher mentions the high interest area during the student's vacuum pause.

Teacher's name _____ Observer _____

Use Action Words Last

When a teacher uses action words such as "take, open, do, make," it activates the students' bodies and they start to move. For example, if the teacher says, "Take out your science books and open to page 95 and look at..." When the students are moving, they are not as able to hear the information accurately. Inadvertently, the teacher has created two groups in the room, those who have their books open to page 95 and those who are lost. In essence, the lesson is slightly out-of-sync. There are a few possible maneuvers the instructor can do to overcome this: the teacher can say the action words last or the teacher can use some kind of a non-verbal gesture (such as our hand raised up in a traffic cop "stop position") to indicate to the class to wait until the teacher has finished the whole message.

The teacher wants feedback on whether the placement of action words in a set of instructions makes a difference in terms of how well the class hears and responds. The teacher will intentionally place the action words at the beginning of the instructions and then, at the end, while using a non-verbal gesture indicating "STOP" as the teacher says the action words. By doing this contrasting placement of the action words, the observer can watch the class' reaction and provide the teacher with the feedback she wants.

The teacher will arrange the lesson so that there are three to four occasions when action words will be used during the observer's ten to fifteen minute stay.

Least Recommended

1. List the action words the teacher said: _____

2. The teacher is intentionally going to place the action word(s) at the beginning of the instructions. List the instructions that followed the action words: _____

_____

3. Describe what percentage of the class responded appropriately: _____

_____

_____

_____

4. Comment on how in sync this segment of the lesson appeared to be: _____

_____

_____

Teacher's name _____ Observer _____

Use Action Words Last

Recommended

First Example

The teacher will non-verbally signal the observer that she will be switching to the recommended approach.

1. List the action word(s) the teacher said: _____

2. Apart from the action word(s), what were the instructions? _____

3. Describe the placement of the action word(s). If a non-verbal gesture was used, what was the gesture and was the signal held until the teacher wanted the class to begin? _____

_____

_____

4. Describe what percentage of the class responded appropriately: _____

5. Comment on how in sync this segment of the lesson appeared to be: _____

_____

_____

Second Example

The teacher will again do the recommended approach.

1. List the action word(s) the teacher said: _____

2. Apart from the action word(s), what were the instructions? _____

3. Describe the placement of the action word(s). If a non-verbal gesture was used, what was the gesture and was the signal held until the teacher wanted the class to begin?

_____

_____

4. Describe what percentage of the class responded appropriately: _____

5. Comment on how in sync this segment of the lesson appeared to be: _____

_____

_____

Discuss the students' attentiveness with where and how the teacher placed the action words. If it were a right-brain day, did the teacher also use the board or overhead to show the specifics of the instructions?

Chapter Nine: Transition to Seatwork

*"A person does not know what he is saying
until he knows what he is not saying."*

G.K. Chesterton

Notes on Specific Skills:

Exit Direction Refinements

The most important aspect of this skill is graphics. Encourage the teacher to develop them. The skill of "silently pointing" will be fully appreciated in light of what *Influence Approach* presented. The concept of trying to break the negative reinforcement syndrome is the common goal of both "silently pointing" and *Influence Approach*. We want the student to get no attention when she is being inappropriate.

Advanced Exit Directions

This is a clever skill that takes very little time. Encourage all elementary teachers to do this technique.

Maintaining the Productive Atmosphere

Far and away the *Mini MITS* is the most powerful technique of the three techniques listed. *Mini MITS* applies to all grade levels. A teacher can use it every day during seatwork. It is a technique whose influence is increased by the frequency of its use. *Private Voice* and *Walking Speed* are really important for non-visual teachers to practice; encourage them.

Gender Reminder

When applicable, the teacher is referred to with the male pronoun and the student with the female pronoun.

Teacher's name _____ Observer _____

Exit Direction Refinements

From *Exit Directions*, the teacher has learned to

- visually display directions,

- consistently use a certain location and systematically use colors,

- laminate those that are used on a regular basis.

The teacher would now like feedback on his implementation of some additional techniques related to *Exit Directions*. Because of the nature of these skills, you, the observer, will be asked to visit several times. Each stay will be very short, just during the actual exit directions. Each time the teacher will indicate which of the several techniques below he wants feedback on for that particular visit. The teacher will fill out all 1's and 2's before the observation.

Silently Point

It would be unrealistic for us to think that students can switch overnight from the previous format of asking the teacher to repeat the *Exit Directions* during seatwork to actually reading them from the board. During Seatwork, when the pupils ask questions that are answered on the board (e.g., "What do I do next?"), the teacher has been practicing pointing to the board in silence. It is very important for the teacher to do this without having eye contact with the student who is asking. The teacher wants to avoid eye contact so that the student does not perceive this as a way of getting attention from the teacher. This technique will need to be observed during the days that the teacher is making the transition from oral *Exit Directions* to visual *Exit Directions*.

1. Date of observation: _____

2. Initials and location of certain students the teacher wants the observer to especially watch to see if they are assisted by the teacher silently pointing: _____

_____

3. If a student asks about information that is listed on the board, the teacher will silently point to the board. The observer will describe the specifics of how the teacher pointed without giving eye contact. Also mention the student's reactions: _____

_____

_____

_____

Teacher's name _____ Observer _____

Exit Direction Refinements

Queries

When the teacher announces the *Exit Directions* and shows them on the board or laminated card and asks, "Any questions?" it is recommended that the teacher write the additional information on the board as he responds to their queries; otherwise, he will probably give the same oral information several more times.

1. Date of observation: _____

2. Initials and location of certain students the teacher wants the observer to especially watch to see if they are assisted by the teacher answering queries visually as well as orally:

_____

_____

3. The teacher will do the least recommended approach—just orally answer questions. The observer will describe the students' (listed in 2) attentiveness and understanding of what to do. Also, mention if the teacher had to repeat the additional information: _____

_____

_____

4. Either while doing this same lesson or during another lesson with *Exit Directions* of equivalent length and complexity, the teacher will do the recommended approach by writing the specifics of the additional information. The observer will watch these same students' change in attentiveness and clarity of what to do. Also note if there was a decrease in the number of times the teacher had to repeat the additional information: _____

_____

Graphics

The right-brain students tend to pay more attention to graphics, symbols and real objects instead of words. As much as possible, the teacher wants to include these on his laminated cards and when he writes on the board. For example, the teacher could use a laminated cover of the workbook and write the page and problem numbers on or near the cover.

1. Date of observation: _____

2. Initials and location of certain students the teacher wants the observer to especially watch to see if they are assisted by the graphics: _____

_____

Teacher's name _____ Observer _____

Exit Direction Refinements

3. To test the axiom, the teacher will intentionally not use any graphics but show the directions in sentences. Describe the students (those listed in 2) attentiveness and understanding of what to do: _____

_____

4. Either while doing this same lesson with *Exit Directions* or during another lesson with *Exit Directions* of equivalent length and complexity, the teacher will use graphics. The observer will watch these same students change in attentiveness and understanding of what to do: _____

_____

Hidden and Then Exposed

In classrooms where the teacher posts the *Exit Directions* before or during the lecture, some students will start doing them during the teacher's presentation. There are advantages to keeping the directions hidden until you have finished the Teaching portion of the lesson is finished and it is time to release the class to begin their seatwork or homework.

1. Date of observation: _____

2. List the initials and location of certain students the teacher wants the observer to especially watch to see if they are assisted by the directions being hidden and then exposed. Up to now, the observer has been watching our kinesthetic students. For this activity, the students the observer may be watching might be the "better" visual students: _____

_____

3. To test this axiom, the teacher will intentionally have the *Exit Directions* exposed throughout the lesson. The observer will describe if the students (listed in 2) begin doing the directions early. _____

4. Either while doing this same lesson with *Exit Directions* or during another lesson with *Exit Directions* of equivalent length and complexity, the teacher will wait until the *Exit Directions* are given before exposing the visual representation of the directions. The observer will describe the students' (listed in 2) reaction to seeing the directions at the time they are exposed: _____

_____

Teacher's name _____ Observer _____

Advanced Exit Directions

When the class is on task and the teacher sees someone behaving inappropriately, he wants to shift the student toward being on task as silently as possible. The silence maintains the productive atmosphere. The *Exit Directions* allow the minimal verbal communication. *Advanced Exit Directions* is a process of numbering the directions on the board. This will allow the teacher to put a student on task during Seatwork by silently referring to particular parts of the *Exit Directions*.

The teacher provides the observer a seating chart with the students circled who most

likely will need to be reminded to stay on task. We want to especially focus on whether the teacher is able to remain silent when putting these students back on task by using non-verbal signals as often as possible. It is suggested that the teacher indicate to the observer before the observation what some of the non-verbal signals that will be used. The observer will stay for ten to fifteen minutes during the Seatwork phase of the lesson. It is recommended that the observer arrive sometime just before the *Exit Directions* are given.

First Example

The first example of the teacher putting the student back on task.

Date of observation _____ Time of day _____

1. Student's initials or description who was put ON task: _____

2. Non-verbal signal used by teacher _____

_____

3. Reaction of student _____

_____

_____

4. Did the teacher wait until the student went ON task and had breathed at least twice before the teacher resumed whatever the teacher was doing? **Yes/No**

5. Were students who were ON task oblivious to the maneuver? **Yes/No**

6. Describe the ON task students' reactions or lack of reactions to the teacher using *Advanced Exit Directions*: _____

_____

Advanced Exit Directions

Second Example

1. Student's initials or description who was put ON task: _____

2. Non-verbal signal used by teacher _____

_____

3. Reaction of student _____

_____

4. Did the teacher wait until the student went ON task and had breathed at least twice before the teacher resumed whatever the teacher was doing? **Yes/No**

5. Were students who were on task oblivious to the maneuver? **Yes/No**

6. Describe the ON task students' reactions or lack of reactions to the teacher using *Advanced Exit Directions*: _____

_____

Third Example

1. Student's initials or description who was put ON task: _____

2. Non-verbal signals used by teacher _____

_____

3. Reaction of student _____

_____

4. Did the teacher wait until the student went ON task and had breathed at least twice before the teacher resumed whatever the teacher was doing? **Yes/No**

5. Were students who were on task oblivious to the maneuver? **Yes/No**

6. Describe the ON task students' reactions or lack of reactions to the teacher using *Advanced Exit Directions*: _____

_____

Maintaining the Productive Atmosphere
Private Voice

We know that more productive seatwork occurs because of a visual atmosphere that starts with the teacher doing visual *Exit Directions* and *MITS*. How is this atmosphere maintained and fostered once the *Most Important Twenty Seconds* is up? This skillsheet will cover one of the three factors that is conducive to maintaining the productive motif.

Public vs. Private Voice

Students have been conditioned over their school career to respond to the teacher's call for attention. The teacher knows that this request can be both verbally done (e.g., "Class," "Boys and girls," "Gang," "Quiet please," "Look this way," etc.) and non-verbally. One of the primary ways pupils are non-verbally signaled to give the instructor attention is the teacher's voice. It is imperative that the teacher pay attention to whether he is using a "public" or "private" voice. The teacher wants to do the former during presentations and the latter during Seatwork time.

To test this contention, the teacher will, during Seatwork, do the opposite: use the public lecture voice while assisting a student one-on-one. As an observer, notice how students tend to shift their bodies when the teacher uses his public voice. Some possibilities:

Least Recommended

- The teacher's public voice will be like a stone in a pond with reverberations of students' movement.

- The teacher's public voice will initially produce ripples of movement and then a freeze.

- At other times, the observer might see the students' bodies shift halfway through the teacher's comment or perhaps at the end of the remark.

- At other times, those students close to the teacher will freeze and those farther away may move.

- And if the teacher's voice is angry and loud, the students often freeze like frightened animals.

Teacher's name _____ Observer _____

Maintaining the Productive Atmosphere

Public Voice

1. **First example** of teacher using a "teaching voice."

    Observer's description of the teacher's voice pattern in terms of volume and length of speaking: _____

    _____

    Description of the students' reactions; specifically when they start to shift and when did they stop and if certain sections of the room were more affected than others: _____

    _____

    _____

2. **Second example** of teacher using a teaching voice.

    Observer's description of the teacher's voice pattern in terms of volume, length, etc.

    _____

    _____

    Description of the students' reactions; specifically, when they start to shift, when do they stop and if certain sections of the room are more affected than others: _____

    _____

    _____

Private Voice

    As planned, the teacher will non-verbally signal the observer that the teacher will do the recommended approach of using a private voice while helping students one-on-one. The observer will notice, hopefully, the students not shifting their bodies. Description of the shifts or lack of them: _____

    _____

    _____

    _____

Teacher's name _____ Observer_____

Maintaining the Productive Atmosphere
Walking Speed

In *Maintaining the Productive Atmosphere: Private Voice*, the teacher explored the effect his voice had on the class' concentration. This skill's focus is on the consequence of the teacher's walking speed as he moves about the room assisting students one-on-one. When a teacher walks too fast around the room, he is like a *boat going through water*; there is a *wake* behind him.

To test the validity of this aphorism, the teacher will first do the opposite and then the recommended style. The teacher will cue the observer as to when he will intentionally move rapidly from one side of the room to the other side.

Least Recommended

1. Observer's description of where the teacher moved to and from and the speed:

_____

2. Description of the effect it had on the students. Be specific as to whether those students most affected were closer or farther away from the path of the teacher. Especially pay attention to the kinesthetic learners (Attention Deficit Disorder/Hyperactive/etc.): _____

_____

The teacher may want to do the above more than once because the cumulative effect of the wake is geometric. Picture a wake hitting the shore of a pond and then bouncing off the shore to clash with the next set of ripples that are coming from the next passage of the speedboat.

Recommended

3. The teacher cues that he is switching to a calmer, slower movement pattern. Observer's description of the effects and, hopefully, the lack of ripples on the students' ability to concentrate: _____

_____

Summarize the effects the teacher's walking speed behaviors had on the students' productivity, especially the kinesthetic learners: _____

_____

_____

_____

Maintaining the Productive Atmosphere
Mini MITS

From previous chapters we know that when we make the transition into seatwork by *Visual Directions* and do the *Most Important Twenty Seconds* pause, we have, at least initially, more productivity from the class. In *Maintaining the Productive Atmosphere: Private Voice* and *Walking Speed,* we covered two variables that maintain the atmosphere: using a private voice and moving around the room slowly. This skill is a combination of these two.

Since the teacher's non-verbal communication is the key to management and since the PAUSE is the single most influential non-verbal signal, we have to figure out how to do the PAUSE frequently. Some rules of thumb:

- Every time the teacher uses his public teaching voice, he wants to do a full *MITS* or at least a *Mini MITS* (e.g., five seconds instead of twenty).

- After every second or third student the teacher assists, he will stand, breathe and look at the class in general.

To test the effectiveness of these axioms, the teacher will do the opposite of the suggested way. This way you, the observer, can give the teacher feedback on the students' responses.

Least Recommended

1. As the observer, describe how the teacher during seatwork intentionally makes an announcement and then, using a public voice, immediately moves to help a student. Describe the ripple effect this maneuver has on the class: _____

_____

The teacher may want to do this several times to notice the cumulative effect the announcements without a PAUSE have on the class.

Recommended

2. During this same seatwork time period, the teacher will make an announcement in the recommended way:

- Getting their attention (remembering to speak just above their collective volume, then PAUSING and dropping the voice).

- Making the announcement dragging his voice by slowly emphasizing the words at the end of the sentence.

- PAUSING (full or *Mini MITS*), then slowly helping another student.

Teacher's name _____ Observer _____

Maintaining the Productive Atmosphere

Description of 2 on the previous page: _____

_____

Description of the effect of 2 compared to 1 on the previous page: _____

_____

Recommended

As the teacher finishes helping every second or third student, does he stand up straight, look around at the class and breathe? This *MITS*, even when the teacher hasn't made an announcement, results in the class settling down. There are several factors to consider:

• Is this stand, breathe and look being done after every second, third or fourth student? The key is how often the class needs to be settled down.

• Is the teacher facing the class when he stands, breathes and looks?

• Is the teacher non-verbally signaling the next student that he will be there in a minute to help? Sometimes, the teacher will try to cue a student without looking at the student.

1. Describe the class signals that the teacher pays attention to in determining the frequency of the maneuver: _____

_____

2. As the teacher did the Stand, Breathe and Look, describe where the teacher looked and for how long: _____

_____

3. Describe how the teacher is non-verbally signaling the next student that he will help and will be there in a minute. Is he able to do so without looking? _____

_____

4. Describe the effects of the above process as to how the class settles down. Also, notice if the teacher's stress level has decreased and the energy level is higher for both the teacher and students: _____

_____

Mouse Doodles

Be ambitious enough to be patient.
Practice one skill a week.

Nylon was finally realized in 1939—12 years after its conception. The ball point pen was first conceived in 1938. When did it finally come to fruition?

Chapter Ten: Seatwork

*"The influence of power is short-lived
while the power of influence is endless."*

While Chapters Seven through Ten are elaborations of the skills introduced in Chapter Six, this is even more true of Chapter Ten than it is of the other chapters. Make sure the teacher has the *OFF/Neutral/ON* and *Influence Approach* skills perfected before tackling Chapter Ten skills. These skills are the most sophisticated techniques of all thirty-one skills. Chapter Ten validates both the necessity of and the actual ingredients of POWER. Chapter Ten also puts POWER in a context of when and how much to use it.

Since ENVoY is about non-verbal management, the major focus has been on the teacher interacting with the class as a whole. This chapter emphasizes the instructor's contact with students on a one-on-one basis. Keep in mind that ENVoY is only viewing the non-verbal management aspects of the teacher-student interchange. Other educational perspectives must also be considered. The purpose of managing is to take the student who is OFF task to working successfully (ON task). If we don't have work he can be engaged in, then we manage full time because the student can only go from OFF task to Neutral and then he goes back to OFF task. As mentioned earlier, effective management comes about only when we can manage the students into an appropriate curriculum. While ENVoY magnifies the teacher involvement in management, this manual is one tube of the educational bin-

oculars—the other tube is the consideration from the curriculum perspective.

Notes on Specific Skills: Power to Influence Approach

Encourage the teacher to do the *Power to Influence Overview* several times because Vacuum Pauses are an elusive phenomenon. As a coach, you may want to arrange to have the teacher and you jointly do the Observation Skills. You may advise the teacher to try to do the Inventions only after Vacuum Pauses have been observed.

OFF/Neutral/ON Refinements

The skill has two parts: "Dot-to-Dot" and "Two Stage Exiting." The first section offers a philosophical template of how to categorize students. If the teacher is offended, modify or skip it altogether. ENVoY is intended to be an educational smorgasbord with each reader selecting only those items that match the teacher's palate.

Positive Reinforcement: One-on-One

This skill can be employed during the Teaching phase as well as during Seatwork. *Group Feedback* is very similar to all other visual-oriented techniques: *Opening Visual Instructions, Exit Directions, Exit Direction*

Refinements, Advanced Exit Directions. Because *Group Feedback* can also be used during the Teaching phase, all the phases of a lesson can benefit from the teacher being visual. The use of the visual mode greatly increases the teacher's employment of her non-verbal messages because what the teacher might verbally say is represented visually. Encourage the teacher to use visuals a lot and to laminate the directions most routinely utilized.

3 Before Me

This is an outstanding skill for elementary teachers.

Phantom Hand

Encourage the teacher to have successfully completed "Two Stage Exiting" from *OFF/Neutral/ON Refinements* before broaching this skill. Make sure you and the teacher simulate this skill before attempting it in the classroom. *Phantom Hand* and Vacuum Pause are the two most sophisticated ENVoY skills, with the *Power to Influence Approach* skill closely following them.

Gender Reminder

When applicable, the teacher is referred to with the female pronoun and the student with the male pronoun.

Power to Influence Approach

With most of the ENVoY skills, it is suggested that the teacher learn the techniques by practicing with marginal students because it is easier for the teacher to practice her timing. With the average student, the teacher can use the Indirect approach of *Influence* to get a student to use appropriate behavior. This skill focuses on the teacher working with the "worst case scenario" students. With them, the gentleness of the *Influence Approach* is often too subtle. The teacher often has to resort to *Power* to get their attention. The difficulty with the teacher using this *Power Approach* with the "worst case" student is that the teacher runs the risk of getting stuck being a cop. The teacher wants to use *Power* to shake the student from OFF to Neutral and then do a *Break & Breathe* and shift to the *Influence Approach* as she indirectly has the student move from Neutral to ON.

Patience

Because of the sophistication of these skills, we ask the observer to have completed the following sections before proceeding with this skill:

- *OFF/Neutral/ON*—both self and peer forms

- *Influence Approach*—both self and peer forms

- *Decontamination of the Classroom*— self form

- *Break & Breathe*—self form

- *Power to Influence Approach*—self form

By doing the above-mentioned prerequisite exercises, the observer will have the knowledge and ability to give the teacher feedback when the teacher does the following skills:

- Recognition of OFF vs. Neutral vs. ON task

- The difference between Power = Direct vs. Influence = Indirect.

- Sorting mental states by locations

- The role of breathing in all of the above

Power to Influence Approach

Overview

We are presuming that the indirect approach wasn't effective. The extreme right-brain kinesthetic student is a member of the ESP Club = Earth as a Second Planet. If the teacher approaches too subtly, the student remains gone. Therefore, the teacher is going to do the *Power to Influence Approach*. The teacher will be using some or all of the non-verbal components of the Direct/Power Approach:

Power Approach
- Teacher approaches from the front
- Teacher makes eye contact
- Teacher is breathing high and shallow
- Teacher is close, maybe touching the student
- Teacher is verbal, perhaps using a loud voice

The teacher will, of course, be doing one continuous intervention while the questions that follow delineate the stages separately.

Once the teacher has the student's attention (the pupil is in Neutral), the teacher wants to change to the Indirect Approach of Influence. The teacher does this by deleting any non-verbal signals that are person-to-person. This includes stopping any eye contact, high and shallow breathing, touch, harsh or loud voice, etc. Instead, the teacher will change to a person-to-content emphasis.

Influence Approach
- Moving to the student's side
- Looking at the workbook on the student's desk
- Breathing low and full
- Being farther away from the student
- Either using no voice or a whisper

This switching from a disciplinary persona to a teaching persona is basically what the teacher did when we observed *ABOVE (Pause) Whisper*.

Teacher's name _____ Observer _____

Power to Influence Approach

1. **First student's** initials or description of: _____

2. The teacher will approach the student indirectly. Describe what happened: _____

_____

3. Describe which aspects of the *Power Approach* the teacher used: _____

_____

Describe what the teacher might have noticed that indicated that the student had come back to earth and was in a Neutral state so that the teacher could stop the *Power Approach*:

_____

Describe the teacher's *Break & Breathe:* _____

4. Describe which aspects of the *Influence Approach* the teacher used: _____

_____

5. Describe the beneficial results for the teacher and the student: _____

_____

1. **Second student's** initials or description of: _____

2. The teacher will approach the student indirectly. Describe what happened: _____

_____

3. Describe which aspects of the *Power Approach* the teacher used: _____

_____

Describe what the teacher might have noticed that indicated that the student had come back to earth and was in a Neutral state so the teacher could stop the *Power Approach*:

_____

Describe the teacher's *Break & Breathe*: _____

4. Describe which aspects of the *Influence Approach* the teacher used: _____

_____

5. Describe the beneficial results for the teacher and the student: _____

_____

Power to Influence Approach

Observational Skills

As an observer, you have provided the teacher with feedback on doing the Power intervention to get the student to Neutral and then switching to the Influence intervention to get the student to ON task. The teacher wants feedback on a most subtle and yet powerful skill—intervening at a specific time. The contention is that an OFF task kinesthetic student has the following possible behaviors:

Hyperactive Characteristics

- impulsive and very, very quick

- concentration spans are extremely short

- doesn't focus well or long

- is above average intelligence

- externally oriented with high distractibility tendencies

Because of these propensities, the student doesn't stay ON or OFF task on the same thing long. He is like a fly that randomly buzzes from one external object to another.

The teacher has visited another teacher's classroom to practice observing the following behaviors: the student tends to have one focus, then a brief pause of "no focus" and then on to another focus. We have labeled the brief pause a vacuum pause. This is due to a void where nothing is happening. What is the advantage of noticing vacuum pauses? 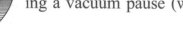 Previously the teacher has been doing a two-step intervention, getting the student from OFF to Neutral and then from Neutral to ON. Intervening during a vacuum pause (which is an in-

nate Neutral) saves a step. Because of the sophistication of the skill, make sure you have filled in the "Observational Skills" of the self form before proceeding. This observational training is a prerequisite in order for the observer to have the necessary perceptual skills to notice and to give the teacher feedback on this timing technique.

Interventions

There are a variety of interventions that can be done at the student's vacuum pause.

Visual: catching the student's attention via eye contact

Auditory: getting the student's attention by saying his name or clearing your throat or making a sound.

Kinesthetic: moving toward the student or touching him to get his attention.

The difficulty is timing. When the teacher sees the student in a vacuum pause and then starts to intervene, enough time has elapsed so that the student is no longer at the vacuum pause but now is OFF task on a new focus. The teacher literally misses the vacuum pause between the time gap of "when the teacher saw" and "when the teacher did." Therefore, the teacher needs to notice the rhythm or frequency as to how often the vacuum pause comes. Also, the student usually shows indications that he is nearing the end of one focus so that the teacher can anticipate that the vacuum pause is coming. This allows the teacher to start her intervention (e.g., look at, say name, touch, etc.) toward the end of one focus and by the time the teacher does the intervention, the teacher is at the student's vacuum pause.

Teacher's name _____ Observer _____

Power to Influence Approach

The teacher will arrange to have the observer visit her classroom during the Seatwork phase of a lesson when it will be highly likely that some extreme kinesthetic students will be acting as though they are members of the ESP Club: Earth as a Second Planet. The teacher will do interventions with these pupils during their vacuum pauses. What is great about the teacher practicing this skill is that even if the teacher aims for a vacuum pause and instead gets a focus, the teacher is learning about timing. As with most perceptual training, there is no failure, only feedback. As long as the teacher is able to intervene at the vacuum pause occasionally, the teacher will be convinced of the effectiveness of timing and therefore be motivated to continue to practice. The teacher has the choice of selecting the same students.

Intervening at Vacuum Pause

1. **Third student's** initials or description of: _____

2. As an observer, describe your sense of the student's frequency of being on one focus, then the vacuum pause and then buzzing to another focus. How long was each focus?

_____

3. Describe what the specific signs were that the teacher might be noticing that indicates that the student was nearing the end of one focus and about to enter the vacuum pause:

_____

_____

4. Describe the style of intervention the teacher used (visual, auditory, kinesthetic or a combination): _____

_____

_____

5. This next question will take practice on your part to answer as an observer. Did the teacher intervene at the vacuum pause, near the vacuum pause or during a focus? _____

_____

6. Think about the teacher's maneuvering. In other words, if the intervention was successfully done at the student's vacuum pause, did the teacher immediately switch to the Influence Approach? If so, describe details. If the intervention was not done during the student's vacuum pause, reflect on the components of the Direct Approach of Power that were used.

Teacher's name _____ Observer _____

Power to Influence Approach

Intervening at Vacuum Pause

1. **Fourth student's** initials or description of: _____

2. As an observer, describe your sense of the student's frequency of being on one focus, then the vacuum pause and then buzzing to another focus. How long was each focus?

    _____

    _____

3. Describe what the specific signs were that the teacher might be noticing that indicates that the student was nearing the end of one focus and about to enter the vacuum pause:

    _____

    _____

4. Describe the style of intervention the teacher used (visual, auditory, kinesthetic or a combination): _____

    _____

    _____

5. This next question will take practice on your part to answer as an observer. Did the teacher intervene at the vacuum pause, near the vacuum pause or during a focus? _____

    _____

6. Dialogue with the teacher about the maneuvers. In other words, if the intervention was successfully done at the student's vacuum pause, did the teacher immediately switch to the Indirect Approach of Influence? If so, describe details. If the intervention was not done during the student's vacuum pause, describe and discuss the components of the Direct Approach of Power that were used: _____

    _____

    _____

    _____

    _____

OFF/Neutral/ON Refinements

As an observer, it is essential that you know that ENVoY's Seatwork skills have evolved from:

- the *Influence Approach*

- making sure the student is ON task as the teacher leaves him

Make sure, as observer, that you know these skills from Chapters One and Six.

For the *OFF/Neutral/ON Refinements*, we will cover two concepts: Dot-to-Dot and Two Stage Exiting. Because of the sophistication of the skills the teacher is incorporating, you will be asked to make several visits in order to provide the teacher with the feedback needed to have incremental progress.

Dot-to-Dot

On days when the teacher feels like she is spinning her wheels, she is trying to handle the seatwork productivity in a manner that can be labeled "dot-to-dot." Remember, as a child, the drawing books with blank pages except for numbers with dots next to them? We would trace from one number's dot to the next. Well, on days when the teacher is frantic, she tends to race around from one student who is OFF task to another. If a video camera was centered on the classroom ceiling and the tape was reviewed at the fast forward speed, the observer could see the teacher going dot-to-dot with certain students. The difference between the drawing book and the video is that the former makes a picture that makes sense.

Inventory:

For seatwork purposes, the teacher has categorized her students into three groups that she has contact with:

Group H students—those students the teacher just Helps but doesn't have to put on task. Their initials are: _____ , _____ , _____ , _____ and _____ .

Group H & M students—those that the teacher both Helps and has to Manage from time to time. Their initials are:_____ , _____ , _____ , _____ and _____ .

Group M students—those who require a lot of Management; the teacher's primary interaction with them is Managing. Their initials are: _____ , _____ , _____ , _____ , _____ , _____ , _____ .

As an observer, visit the teacher's classroom at least two, and preferably, three times during the Seatwork phase of a lesson. Provide the teacher feedback as to whether the teacher is actually having contact with the students in the above categories. One way of doing this is to have the teacher provide a seating chart and color code the locations of each group. For example, Group H students could be underlined in red; Group H & M students are underlined in blue and Group M students in green. The observer can put an "H" every time the teacher helps a student and an "M" next to students that the teacher manages.

Teacher's name _____ Observer _____

OFF/Neutral/ON Refinements

After two or three visits of fifteen minutes each, the chart might show if the Group H students just have "H's" next to their names; Group H & M students have "H's" and "M's" next to their names and, likewise, Group M students only have "M's" next to their names.

Suggestions

The teacher will know her circumstances much better than any generalized theory, so, the following are only guidelines that the teacher can consider having the observer follow. The teacher may modify the guidelines in any way she wants.

Group H students: Those are the students the teacher helps one-on-one. This is the classification of students the teacher wants to help. Sometimes it is so frustrating that teachers can't do what they love to do—

teach. Teachers love to impart, assist and facilitate others. Of course, this whole ENVoY book is intended to make us more effective in our management skills so that we can spend more time giving.

The teacher is practicing accepting the fact that she is a part of a system that often cannot sufficiently serve the Group H students. Give the teacher feedback on whether she seems relaxed while helping these students or, more importantly, when the teacher cannot help these students because she is spending time putting other students back on task. If the teacher is ambitious enough, she will invite you in on the days when she knows she will have to spend more seatwork time managing them than actually helping. Our profession needs teachers with big hearts who also know how to take care of themselves. Watch the teacher during the seatwork time on a day that is other than a "good" day.

Write your notes about what the teacher is doing. Especially pay attention to whether the teacher is breathing abdominally and calmly or high and in sighs. _____

_____

_____

When you debrief, you are basically asking these questions:

• What do you have control over?

• What do you not have control over?

• What would it take to accept the conditions you don't have control over?

As the observer, nonjudgmentally write out the teacher's responses: _____

_____

_____

Teacher's name _____ Observer _____

OFF/Neutral/On Refinements

Group H & M students: These are the students the teacher has been both helping and managing. The teacher has been noticing if there is a correlation between her helping these students and whether they increase their on-task behavior. In other words, are some Group H & M students misbehaving because they are unable to academically involve themselves? If so, the teacher doesn't want to attempt the *Influence Approach* because it won't work. Instead, the teacher wants to go directly over and help the Group H & M students as soon as possible after she has released the class (*Exit Directions* and *MITS)*. If the teacher cannot go to the Group H & M students, the teacher is trying to accept the possibility that these students will not be on task. The teacher is temporarily considering these Group H & M students as Group M students. And the axiom for the Group M students is: are these students bothering others? If not, and if you don't have the time, then let the students be. As an observer, give the teacher feedback on the following:

- is the teacher either directly approaching these Group H & M students or

- checking to see if their off-task behaviors are interfering with others' learning?

  • If yes, intervene.

  • If not, leave them alone.

As the observer, nonjudgmentally write out the teacher's responses: _____

_____

_____

Group M students: These are the pupils the teacher mostly manages and spends very little time helping. The teacher has reflected on whether she is putting them on task:

- for their own good

- or because their off-task behavior is interfering with others' learning.

Our profession is famous for doing things because of a philosophical consideration we believe in, even if it is less than effective use of our time and energy. As observer, give the teacher feedback on whether the teacher is intervening only with those Group M students who are interfering with others' learning. Remember, it is not that we want to ignore the Group M students who are off task and not bothering others, it is just that the teacher has a limited amount of time and energy and has to be selective.

Your notes on observation of teacher's responses (or lack of response) to Group M students: _____

_____

_____

Teacher's name _____ Observer _____

OFF/Neutral/ON Refinements

Summary of dot-to-dot

The teacher has categorized some of the pupils into three categories:

• Group H—students the teacher helps

• Group H & M—students the teacher both helps and manages

• Group P—students whom the teacher mainly manages

The teacher's purpose in practicing these skills is to prevent racing around her room in a dot-to-dot fashion. The teacher has a limited amount of time and energy during seatwork. She has to prioritize. The suggestions have been to help Group H and H & M students first. Distinguish between those Group M students who are interfering with others' learning and if so, intervene. For those students who are not on task and are not bothering others, leave them alone unless the teacher has the time.

Observer's suggestions on how the teacher is implementing these suggestions: _____

_____

_____

_____

Two Stage Exiting

Off/Neutral/ON and *Influence Approach* focus on getting a student from OFF task through Neutral to ON task. Using these skills will change the syndrome of negative contact between the teacher and the at-risk student to positive contact. Now a new problem arises: how to get away from the student. This stems from two causes. Sometimes the student is "contact hungry" and doesn't want the teacher to leave and sometimes the teacher's presence is needed to keep him ON task. In either case, the following skill will be of assistance.

When the student has been ON task for at least two breaths (the pupil has inhaled and exhaled twice):

A. The teacher will slowly position her body so that the teacher is standing upright and next to the student.

B. Since eye contact in a positive situation will usually increase the warmth of the interaction and thereby elicit an interchange, the teacher will keep her eyes on the student's work. This completes the first stage of exiting.

C. The teacher will slowly and gradually step back from the student so that the student cannot see the teacher. The teacher will watch the student to make sure the pupil does remain ON task independent of her.

D. The teacher will slowly and gradually move away from the student.

Teacher's name _____ Observer _____

OFF/Neutral/ON Refinements

Implementation

The letters below correspond to those listed on the previous page.

Exiting

First Student

1. **First student's** initials or description of: _____

   1A. Describe how long it took for the teacher to put herself in an upright position and what it was the teacher saw that indicated the student was breathing fully and was on task:

_____

_____

   1B. Describe how the teacher kept her eyes on the student's work: _____

_____

_____

   1C. Describe how the teacher slowly and gradually stepped back from the student and mention how the student stayed on task. Also mention how long it took and if the teacher had to do any modification because certain conditions occurred: _____

_____

_____

   1D. Describe how the teacher slowly and gradually moved away from the student and mention how the student stayed on task. Also mention how long it took and if the teacher had to do any modification because certain conditions occurred: _____

_____

_____

_____

Teacher's name _____ Observer _____

OFF/Neutral/On Refinements

Exiting

Second Student

2. **Second student's** initials or description of: _____

    2A. Describe how long it took for the teacher to put herself in an upright position and what it was the teacher saw that indicated the student was breathing fully and was on task:

_____

_____

_____

    2B. Describe how the teacher kept her eyes on the student's work: _____

_____

_____

_____

    2C. Describe how the teacher slowly and gradually stepped back from the student and mention how the student stayed on task. Also mention how long it took and if the teacher had to do any modification because certain conditions occurred: _____

_____

_____

_____

    2D. Describe how the teacher slowly and gradually moved away from the student and mention how the student stayed on task. Also mention how long it took and if the teacher had to do any modification because certain conditions occurred: _____

_____

_____

_____

Positive Reinforcement: One-on-One

A survey of educators indicates that when teachers are more "people oriented" than "idea oriented," their energy level is higher and their self-image greater when they give students "positive strokes." Conversely, their energy level and self-image decrease when they discipline. It is obvious that methods that decrease Negative Reinforcement and increase the teacher's use of Positive Reinforcement are most welcome.

Length of Time

Often the difference between a stroke and a reprimand is the *length of time* between strokes. For example, during Seatwork the teacher is at the transparency projector calling students up to demonstrate ability on the overhead screen. The teacher has judiciously placed Sam (a highly kinesthetic student) in the front row to keep him ON task. The teacher does a variety of techniques to interrupt his inappropriate behavior and put him back ON task. The teacher is using a disciplinary response. For about 30 to 40 seconds, Sam stays ON task. The teacher is intervening every 60 to 90 seconds. If the teacher gives positive strokes every 25 seconds, the length of time the student will stay on task often increases and the teacher feels better using positive actions.

Stroking

Another way of looking at switching from "negative interaction" (disciplining) to "positive interaction" (stroking) is each time the teacher does disciplinary intervention, she follows with visual, auditory or kinesthetic praise within 20 to 25 seconds. This assures the teacher that the student knows what behavior the teacher wants and that the student can get attention in a positive way.

This concept is especially true for right-brain students because of these traits:

Right Brain Students
- Person-to-person interaction
- Short attention span
- Distractibility
- Need for immediate reinforcement

The teacher has practiced these suggestions and now wants your feedback on how the teacher is implementing the recommendations and what effect these maneuvers are having on the student. In order to practice the timing of the techniques, the teacher is selecting the marginal students rather than the worst case students. The teacher will arrange an occasion for your visit when it is likely that positive reinforcement is appropriate. Although this skill is located under the Seatwork phase of a lesson, it could equally be placed in the Teaching phase of a lesson.

Positive Reinforcement: One-on-One

First Student

1. First marginal student's initials or description of: _____

2. Observer's description of the student's inappropriate behavior: _____

_____

_____

3. The teacher will do her normal process of disciplinary intervention.

   • How often did the teacher do it (e.g., "every _____ seconds or minutes")?

   • How long does the student stay on task: _____

4. The teacher will now switch and practice this *Positive Reinforcement* technique. Initially the teacher will do her normal process of disciplinary intervention. Then, while the student is still on task, the teacher will praise the student for appropriate behavior.

   • How did the teacher know she could wait as long as she did? In other words, what were the indications the student was still on task but nearing the end of the student's concentration? _____

_____

_____

_____

   • What was the teacher's praise or positive reinforcement? Keep in mind that sometimes non-verbal reinforcements are better than verbal ones: _____

_____

_____

5. Briefly describe the results. Especially notice if the length of the student's ON task behavior increases. _____

_____

_____

_____

Teacher's name _____ Observer _____

Positive Reinforcement: One-on-One

Second Student

1. Second marginal student's initials or description of: _____

2. Observer's description of the student's inappropriate behavior: _____

_____

_____

3. The teacher will again do her normal process of disciplinary intervention.

   • How often did the teacher do it (e.g., "every _____ seconds or minutes")?

   • How long does the student stay on task: _____

4. The teacher will switch and practice this *Positive Reinforcement* technique. Initially, the teacher will do her normal process of disciplinary intervention. Then, while the student is still on task, the teacher will praise the student for appropriate behavior.

   • How did the teacher know she could wait as long as the she did? In other words, what were the indications the student was still on task but nearing the end of the student's concentration? _____

   _____

   _____

   _____

   • What was the teacher's praise or positive reinforcement? Keep in mind that sometimes non-verbal reinforcements are better than verbal ones: _____

   _____

   _____

   _____

5. Briefly describe the results. Especially notice if the length of the student's ON task behavior increases. _____

_____

_____

_____

Positive Reinforcement: Group Feedback

Seatwork time is most productive when the students are both on task and relaxed. If some of the students are other than appropriate, the teacher needs to give them feedback as to what the teacher expects and how the class is doing compared to those expectations. If the teacher gives this feedback orally, the teacher becomes the "traffic cop." When the teacher plays traffic cop, the teacher often needs to stay visibly present and consequently cannot go help students one-on-one. While the traffic cop approach may increase the class' productivity, the teacher has used the *Power Approach*, which means, among other things, that the pupils are not relaxed. The teacher also has increased the likelihood that the students perceive that they need to be on task for the teacher instead of thinking they are self motivated.

In the section, *Positive Reinforcement: One-on-One*, the age-old concept of "catch 'em doing it right" was explored for the one-on-one situations. Applied here, the teacher wants to collectively give students positive strokes while they are still on task but are starting to fade and, at the same time, she would like to use the *Influence Approach*. The by-products of this method include the following: the students think they are motivating themselves, the teacher still gets to help students one-on-one and the pupils are relaxed. The teacher can accomplish giving feedback in silence with visual non-verbal signals. The examples given on pages 143 - 144 work well through fourth grade and have to be somewhat modified for the middle grades and greatly altered for high school.

The teacher has devised a plan to provide the class with visual feedback to reinforce the behavior the teacher wants the class to have. As the observer, give the teacher feedback on the following:

1. Describe the teacher's visual feedback system: _____

_____

_____

2. Describe how the teacher uses it: _____

_____

_____

3. Describe the effects on the class and the advantages: _____

_____

_____

Teacher's name _____ Observer _____

3 Before Me

We know that the best productive environment for seatwork is a "visual" atmosphere and management that is done with a maximum of non-verbal communication. It all begins with the directions being given on the board visually. We also know that seatwork is the time when the teacher can work individually with students. This skill focuses on how to increase students' independence in knowing what they are to do.

The more they are independent, the more time the teacher will have to assist other students. This skill is designed for students from kindergarten through fifth grade.

The teacher meets with a colleague who will observe. The teacher shares the "3 Before Me" chart and how she plans to use it today with particular refinements she wants feedback on.

1. The poster says: _____

_____

_____

2. Any particulars that the observed teacher wants special feedback on (e.g., a particular student, etc.)? _____

_____

_____

3. Did the teacher do non-verbal hand signals from the chart? As an observer, especially assist the teacher in three areas:

• Was the non-verbal signal done slowly and nonjudgmentally?   **Yes/No**

• Was the process done with minimal interruption to the student the teacher was assisting when another approached? The reason this is so important is that a student might be psychologically so hungry for contact that the student is willing to get in trouble just to have contact.   **Yes/No**

• Describe if any of the students approach with a non-verbal signal (e.g., showing three fingers) indicating he had done *3 Before Me* and was appropriately seeking the teacher's help? It is hoped that the teacher respectfully finished the interaction with the student that the teacher was with before the second student was given attention. _____

_____

_____

_____

Teacher's name _____ Observer _____

Phantom Hand

We know that a kinesthetic student often operates as if he needs the teacher's presence to stay on task during seatwork. As much as the student wants to have individual "papal visits," the teacher needs to assist and monitor all of her students. The question arises, "How does the teacher make her presence known (in a positive way) from a distance?"

In answer to this question, we are presuming the teacher and observer have done *Influence Approach*; therefore, you, as the observer, know the importance of and can recognize a teacher approaching a student when the student is ON task so that the teacher's presence is a "positive contact." This skill is designed for the observer to give the teacher feedback on her ability to leave the student with positive contact and still have the teacher's presence felt after the teacher has left. Because of the sophistication of these perceptual skills, make sure you, the observer, have done the self form of the *Phantom Hand*. This assures that you, as observer, have practiced the following four parts of the *Phantom Hand* in a simulated role with a colleague and also in your own classroom with students:

- Increase touch

- Decrease touch

- Lift off

- Exiting

The teacher will arrange to have the observer visit during the seatwork phase of a lesson.

First student's initials or description of:_____

1. Description of how the teacher moved this student from OFF to ON task: _____

_____

2. Did the teacher keep HER TORSO and, ESPECIALLY, HER FEET STILL while LOOKING at the STUDENT'S WORK? _____

3. Did the teacher do the following? (You may have to surmise some of the items.)

Increase Touch

_____ original touch with fingers spread

_____ initial increase

_____ additional increase

Decrease Touch

_____ decrease from "additional increase" back to the "initial increase" level of contact

_____ decrease from "initial increase" back to the "original touch" level of contact

_____ *g r a d u a l l y* lift hand from contact to barely touching

---

Teacher's name _____ Observer _____

Phantom Hand

Lift Off

_____ *g r a d u a l l y* lift hand from barely touching to being half inch from contact

_____ *g r a d u a l l y* lift hand from half inch to a foot away from contact point

_____ *g r a d u a l l y* drop her hand to her side

Exiting

_____ *s l o w l y* exit from student so he cannot easily see the teacher

Description of the results of the teacher doing *Phantom Hand* (e.g., How long did the student stay on task, etc.) _____

_____

_____

_____

Second student's initials or description of: _____

1. Description of how the teacher moved this student from OFF to ON task. _____

_____

_____

_____

2. Did the teacher keep HER TORSO and, ESPECIALLY, HER FEET STILL while LOOKING at the STUDENT'S WORK? _____

3. Did the teacher do the following? (You may have to surmise some of the items.)

Increase Touch

_____ original touch with fingers spread

_____ initial increase

_____ additional increase

Decrease Touch

_____ decrease from "additional increase" back to the "initial increase" level of contact

_____ decrease from "initial increase" back to the "original touch" level of contact

_____ *g r a d u a l l y* lift hand from contact to barely touching

Teacher's name _____ Observer _____

Phantom Hand

Lift Off

_____ *g r a d u a l l y* lift hand from barely touching to being half inch from contact

_____ *g r a d u a l l y* lift hand from half inch to a foot away from contact point

_____ *g r a d u a l l y* drop her hand to her side

Exiting

_____ *s l o w l y* exit from student so he cannot easily see the teacher

Discuss the results of the teacher doing *Phantom Hand* (e.g., How long did the student stay on task, etc.)

Optional Activity

The teacher may want to actually do the less effective touch and have you give feedback as to what effect this contact has on the student. To really isolate and test this variable, the teacher will initially do the recommended approach (numbers 1 - 4 below) and then do one of the non-recommended approaches: The teacher will:

1. Indirectly move the student to ON task.

2. Make the "Original Touch."

3. Do the "Initial Increase" of contact.

4. Do the "Additional Increase" of contact.

Then the teacher will do the approach that is not recommended—a release of the touch. This approach will be one of the following:

• The teacher pats the student's back as the teacher moves her feet and leaves. We call this "baby burping."

• The teacher rubs the student's back or lets her hand slide off the student's back. We will call the latter "wiping off" the contact point.

• The teacher moves her feet while withdrawing her hand from the contact point.

One of the above two marginal students' initials: _____

As observer, check off which of the following three "less effective" formats the teacher did:

_____ "Baby burping"

_____ "Wipe off"

_____ Simultaneous release of hand while leaving

Discuss the results: (e.g., How long did the student stay on task compared to the results when the recommended format was used?)

Chapter Eleven

The Last Chapter

Many readers are wise enough to inspect a book by reading the last chapter first. This gives them a summary of the essence of the focus of the text and its personal applications. The final segment is usually a culmination of the rest, but that is true for cognitive works. This is not a book about "knowing" but about "doing." So if you turned to this page as my college son would say, "To scope out the profundity," the chapter you want is Chapter One, "The Seven Gems."

Mouse Doodles

Be ambitious enough to be patient.
Practice one skill a week.

This was one of the shorter examples. The ball-point pen came to fruition in 1945—seven years after it was first conceived. Hybrid corn was first conceived in 1908. When was it finally realized? (Guess you will have to be really patient and wait for ENVoY's sequel.)

APPENDIX

Checklist for the Chapters

The Checklists are intended to be used after the the SELF and PEER forms have been completed. They are a holistic encapsulation of ENVoY's concepts. They are written in the third person "Teacher" and can easily be used by the instructor on him or herself as well as by the observer and the evaluator. Not all of the items listed pertain to every lesson nor do they fit every content, educational level or teacher's style of operation.

The checklists are designed so that Chapter One could be used to view an entire lesson with all four phases included. By far, the skills in Chapter One are the seven most important competencies. The four phases of a lesson are addressed individually in Chapters Two through Five in greater detail. The skills from Chapter One will also appear in Chapters Two through Five with their respective phase.

Keeping with the gender equality format of ENVoY, the skills that pertain to the Getting Their Attention and Transition to Seatwork phases will use the male pronoun for the teacher and the female pronoun for the student. Likewise, the phases Teaching and Seatwork will use the female pronoun for the teacher and the male pronoun for the student.

The Seven Gems Checklist

If the person is doing an overview of a whole lesson, then the "Seven Gems" in Chapter One are ideal. Check the items as they are done. Put "N.A." if not applicable. Then use the "comments" area for further details. Our premise is that specific feedback is meaningful and constructive; abstract and nonspecific comments are too judgemental and fluffy to allow the teacher to incorporate the feedback.

Getting Their Attention

Freeze Body

_____ Was the teacher still?

ABOVE (Pause) Whisper

_____ Was the teacher's voice above the collective volume of the class?

_____ Did the teacher p a u s e after the class was attentive?

_____ (optional) Did the teacher do a "step down" as the room gradually quieted?

_____ Did the teacher drop to a whisper after the p a u s e?

Comments: _____

_____

_____

_____

Teaching

Raise Your Hand vs Speak Out

_____ The *Safest Method*: Did the teacher do the verbal and non-verbal signals when initiating each of the following modes?

    _____ Teacher Only One Talking

    _____ Raise Your Hand

    _____ Speak Out the answer

_____ The *Better Maneuver*: Did the teacher eventually drop the verbal level and do just the non-verbal gestures?

_____ The *Ultimate Technique*: With the students responding to the teacher's non-verbal gestures, did the teacher eventually drop the verbal level followed by the drop of the non-verbal level, relying on momentum?

The Seven Gems Checklist

_____ Especially *Be Sensitive When*: If the teacher switched from a mode (e.g., "Speak Out") to a mode to the left of the first mode (e.g., "Raise Your Hand"), did she drop her voice and hold still?

Comments: _____

_____

_____

_____

Transition to Seatwork

Exit Directions

_____ Did the teacher visually display the directions for either seatwork or homework?

_____ Did the teacher display and read the following?

    _____ What was assigned

    _____ How to be done

    _____ When due

    _____ Where to put it when finished

    _____ What the students are to do if they finish the above

_____ Non-verbal Signals: Did the teacher use a systematic location and colored chalk to indicate which of the information on the board pertained to their directions?

_____ Lamination: Did the teacher display some or all of the information in a laminated form?

MITS

_____ Did the teacher read the visual *Exit Directions*?

_____ Did the teacher ask for questions and write any additional information?

_____ Did the teacher verbally release the pupils to begin?

_____ Did the teacher stay still for twenty seconds?

_____ Did the teacher use non-verbal signals to indicate to any student who was asking for help during the twenty seconds that the teacher would help that student in a second?

_____ Did the teacher slowly go help individual students?

Comments: _____

_____

_____

_____

The Seven Gems Checklist

Seatwork

OFF/Neutral/ON

_____ Did the teacher walk slowly when approaching a student who was mildly OFF task?

_____ Did the teacher remain while the student breathed twice as he went from OFF task through Neutral to ON task?

_____ Did the teacher leave the student so that he couldn't see her?

Influence Approach

_____ Did the teacher move toward a student who was mildly OFF task without looking directly at the student?

_____ Did the teacher stop when the student shifted from OFF task to Neutral?

_____ Did the teacher keep the targeted student at least peripherally in front of the teacher?

_____ With the student in a Neutral mental state, if the student started to go back OFF task, did the teacher move more closely and, if appropriate, add some non-verbal components from the Power Approach?

_____ With the student in a Neutral mental state, if the student switched from Neutral to ON task, did the teacher wait until the student had taken two breaths before she went to the student's side to do some form of "positive contact?"

Comments: _____

_____

_____

_____

_____

Getting Their Attention Checklist

Freeze Body

_____ Was the teacher still?

Comments: _____

_____

_____

_____

ABOVE (Pause) Whisper

_____ Was the teacher's voice above the collective volume of the class?

_____ Did the teacher p a u s e after the class was attentive?

_____ (optional) Did the teacher do a "step down" as the room gradually quieted?

_____ Did the teacher drop to a whisper after the p a u s e?

Comments: _____

_____

_____

_____

Freeze Body Refinements

_____ Was the teacher in front of the room when asking the class for their attention?

_____ Did the teacher have his toes pointed ahead?

_____ Did the teacher have his weight evenly on both feet?

_____ Did the teacher use a brief amount of verbiage when asking for the class' attention?

Comments: _____

_____

_____

_____

Opening Visual Instruction

_____ Did the teacher have an academic warm-up activity on the board?

_____ Were the students, on the whole, able to successfully engage in the activity so that you could surmise that the warm-up activity was within their abilities?

Getting Their Attention Checklist

_____ Did the teacher use the board to describe what supplies and materials needed to be out and ready for use?

_____ Did the teacher greet the class and non-verbally direct the students' attention to the instructions on the board?

_____ Did the teacher use laminated posters and signs?

When there is no time Emergency Procedure

_____ The teacher is either not ready for the class or is practicing for such an occasion by pretending to be not ready. In either case, is the teacher writing the directions or instructions on the board as the students enter the classroom?

_____ After the instructions are written, the teacher then gets the pupils' attention. Were his feet still and was there a pause after the teacher's initial remark (which was just above the class's collective loudness)?

Comments: _____

_____

_____

_____

Incomplete Sentences

It is either a right-brain day or the teacher is practicing this skill for a right-brain day.

_____ Did the teacher stop the sentence at the beginning and was it at an unnatural point in the sentence (it is most effective when done inside a word)?

_____ Did the teacher have his voice near or just above the collective volume of the class' noise level?

_____ Did the teacher keep his body still during the phrase and the brief pause that followed the *Incomplete Sentence*?

_____ Did the teacher move his body and breathe after he finished the brief pause that followed the incomplete phrase?

_____ Following the pause, did the teacher lower his volume to a whispery voice and use a slower speed as the sentence is said in its entirety?

Comments: _____

_____

_____

_____

Getting Their Attention Checklist

Positive Comments

_____ Did the teacher use positive comments to reinforce appropriate behaviors?

_____ Did the teacher do the positive comments by acknowledging individuals so that they could be models for others?

_____ Did the teacher use positive comments by acknowledging the group as a unit to reinforce desired behaviors?

_____ Did the teacher operate as if he had strong rapport by using the word "I" (e.g., "I like the way..." or "I appreciate the way...")?

Comments: _____

Decontaminating the Classroom

Because of the nature of this skill, the checklist will include items pertaining to two activities that are in addition to regular teaching: group discipline and one other activity.

When doing group discipline:

_____ Did the teacher leave the following non-verbal aspects of "teaching" at the front of the room when the teacher went to the location for "group discipline."

      _____ chalk

      _____ textbook and papers

      _____ turned off overhead

      _____ face, voice and body posture that is associated with teaching

_____ When the teacher arrived at the "group discipline" location, did the teacher separate getting the class' attention from the message that the teacher delivered?

_____ Did the teacher return to the teaching location and resume the face, voice, body posture and non-verbal communication (e.g. chalk, textbook, papers, etc.).

When doing an activity other than "regular teaching:"

_____ Did the teacher go to a location in the room other than where the teacher normally teaches?

_____ Did the teacher display some non-verbal communication that might be different than what the teacher normally does when doing "routine teaching;" such as a different face, voice, body posturing, use of props?

_____ Did the teacher return to the regular teaching location and resume the face, voice, body posture and other non-verbal communications associated with routine teaching?

Comments: _____

Getting Their Attention Checklist

Break & Breathe

Check which of the following situations the *Break & Breathe* techniques were employed:

_____ Group Discipline

_____ Individual Discipline

_____ Severe *Incomplete Sentence*

_____ Emergency Shout

_____ When the teacher had finished one of the situations above, did the teacher simultaneously shift his body posture and take a deep breath?

_____ Did the teacher then operate with amnesia in terms of the incident that had just occurred? In other words, no references were made to the incident (e.g., "continuing..." etc.)?

_____ Did the teacher resume the verbal and non-verbal communication associated with the new activity and was that new communication different from that displayed during the incident?

Comments: _____

_____

Yellow Light

The pupils are doing independent work. They are not focused on the teacher.

_____ Did the teacher make an announcement that signaled that the time was approaching to direct their attention back to the teacher?

_____ Did the teacher's voice volume allow the students to continue with their focus on the activity they were engaged in?

_____ Did the teacher repeat the announcement?

_____ If the teacher repeated the announcement, did the teacher emphasize the last words in a slow, low, draggy voice?

The teacher is doing the "interactive mode" of the lesson and wants to signal that the time is approaching to switch back to Teacher Only One Talking.

_____ Did the teacher make an announcement that indicated how many more inputs from students would be taken?

_____ Did the teacher's voice volume allow the students to continue with their focus on the activity they were engaged in?

Comments: _____

_____

Teaching Checklist

Raise Your Hand vs. Speak Out

_____ The *Safest Method*: Did the teacher do the verbal and non-verbal signals when initiating each of the following modes?

      _____ Teacher Only One Talking

      _____ Raise Your Hand

      _____ Speak Out the answer

_____ The *Better Maneuver*: When the teacher was in a mode for a while, did the teacher eventually drop the verbal level and do just the non-verbal gestures?

_____ The *Ultimate Technique*: If the teacher was in the same mode long enough, did the teacher eventually drop the verbal level followed by the drop of the non-verbal level, relying on momentum?

_____ *Especially Be Sensitive When*: If the teacher switched from a mode (e.g., "Speak Out") to a mode to the left of the first mode (e.g., "Raise Your Hand"), did she drop her voice and hold still?

Comments: _____

Raise Your Hand vs Speak Out Refinements

When the interest in the content is high:

_____ Did the teacher announce the format to be followed before the content question was asked?

What was the format that the teacher announced?

      _____ Raise your hand

      _____ Call on one student

      _____ Speak out

      _____ Raise your hand then speak out the answer in unison

      _____ Another format:_____

When the interest in the content was low:

_____ Did the teacher say the content question before the format was announced?

What was the format that the teacher announced?

      _____ Raise your hand

      _____ Call on one student

      _____ Speak out

      _____ Raise your hand then speak out the answer in unison

      _____ Another format:_____

Teaching Checklist

Comments: _____

_____

_____

_____

Increasing Non-verbal Signals

The teacher did the new academic non-verbal signals and they mean:

_____ did_____ = _____

_____ did_____ = _____

_____ did_____ = _____

_____ did_____ = _____

The teacher did the new management non-verbal signals and they mean:

_____ did_____ = _____

_____ did_____ = _____

_____ did_____ = _____

_____ did_____ = _____

Comments: _____

_____

_____

_____

Overlap

_____ Before finishing one activity, did the teacher announce the next activity? Did the students get ready for the subsequent activity, then did the teacher resume and finish the previous activity?

_____ Were some or all of the directions for the subsequent activity visually displayed?

_____ Could some or all of the directions be laminated?

Comments (Explore with the teacher if today's overlap technique resulted in more effective ON- task behavior than if the *Overlap* had not been used.): _____

_____

_____

_____

Teaching Checklist

Opposite Side of the Room

_____ Did the teacher move away from a student who raised his hand?

_____ Did the teacher move without looking at the student?

_____ Did the teacher call on a student across the room who did have his hand raised?

Comments: _____

_____

_____

_____

Verbal Rapport With Hard to Reach Students

_____ Does the teacher know at least two items in which the student has a high interest?

_____ Did the teacher say one of the student's items of high interest as the student's attentiveness began to fade?

_____ Did the teacher notice the student looking toward the teacher and then the teacher turned away from the student?

_____ Did the student continue to focus on the teacher?

Comments: _____

_____

_____

_____

Use Action Words Last

_____ Did the teacher announce a set of instructions with the action words being said at the end of the instructions?

_____ Did the teacher announce a set of instructions and use a stop gesture before the action word was said?

_____ Did the teacher visually display the crucial information?

Comments: _____

_____

_____

_____

Transition to Seatwork Checklist

Exit Directions

_____ Did the teacher visually display the directions for either seatwork or homework?

_____ Did the teacher display and read the following?

    _____ What was assigned

    _____ How to be done

    _____ When due

    _____ Where to put it when finished

    _____ What the students are to do if they finish the above

_____ Non-verbal signals: Did the teacher use a systematic location and colored chalk to indicate which of the information on the board pertained to their directions?

_____ Lamination: Did the teacher display some or all of the information in a laminated form?

Comments: _____

_____

_____

_____

MITS

_____ Did the teacher read the visual *Exit Directions*?

_____ Did the teacher ask for questions and write any additional information?

_____ Did the teacher verbally release the pupils to begin?

_____ Did the teacher stay still for twenty seconds?

_____ Did the teacher use non-verbal signals to indicate to any student who was asking for help during the twenty seconds that the teacher would help that student in a second?

_____ Did the teacher slowly go help individual students?

Comments: _____

_____

_____

_____

Transition to Seatwork Checklist

Exit Direction Refinements

Silently Point:

_____ If a student asks the teacher what the student is to do next, did the teacher silently point to the information already written on the board?

_____ Did the teacher avoid or minimize eye contact with the student as the teacher silently pointed to the information on the board?

Queries:

_____ If students asked for information that was not on the board, did the teacher write that information in addition to orally answering the question?

Graphics:

_____ Did the teacher use graphics to assist the right-brain oriented students to understand, remember and follow the exit directions?

Hidden and Then Exposed:

_____ Did the teacher have the exit directions done ahead of time, but hidden? Did the teacher expose the directions when the teacher was ready to explain them?

Comments: _____

_____

_____

_____

Advanced Exit Directions

_____ Did the teacher number the *Exit Directions*?

_____ When a student was OFF task, did the teacher get the student's attention with a minimum of verbiage?

_____ Did the teacher non-verbally ask the student the number of the *Exit Directions* the student was working on?

_____ After the student responded, did the teacher wait until the student went ON task and had breathed at least twice before the teacher resumed whatever the teacher was doing?

_____ While the teacher did this maneuver, did the class remain ON task?

Comments: _____

_____

_____

Transition to Seatwork Checklist

Maintaining the Productive Atmosphere: Private Voice

_____ Did the teacher use a *Private Voice* as the teacher assisted students one-on-one?

Comments: _____

_____

_____

_____

Maintaining the Productive Atmosphere: Walking Speed

_____ Did the teacher walk slowly so that the students were able to concentrate during Seatwork?

Comments: _____

_____

_____

_____

Maintaining the Productive Atmosphere: Mini MITS

_____ If the teacher had to make an announcement during Seatwork, did the teacher get their attention by speaking just above the class' collective voice volume?

_____ As the teacher came to the end of the announcement, did the teacher drag his voice by slowly emphasizing the words at the end of the announcement?

_____ Did the teacher pause after finishing the announcement?

_____ After helping every second to third student, did the teacher stand up straight, look around the class and breathe?

_____ Was the teacher facing the class as the teacher did the Stand, Breathe and Look?

_____ Did the teacher non-verbally signal the next student that he would help in a minute?

Comments: _____

_____

_____

_____

Seatwork Checklist

OFF/Neutral/ON

_____ Did the teacher walk slowly when approaching a student who was mildly OFF task?

_____ Did the teacher remain while the student breathed and went from OFF task through Neutral to ON task?

_____ Did the teacher leave the student so that he couldn't easily see her?

Comments: _____

_____

_____

Influence Approach

_____ Did the teacher move toward a student who was mildly OFF task without looking directly at the student?

_____ Did the teacher stop when the student shifted from OFF task to Neutral?

_____ Did the teacher keep the targeted student at least peripherally in front of the teacher?

_____ With the student in a Neutral mental state, if the student started to go back OFF task, did the teacher move more closely and, if appropriate, add some non-verbal components from the _Power Approach_?

_____ With the student in a Neutral mental state, if the student switched from Neutral to ON task, did the teacher wait until the student had taken two breaths before she went to the student's side to do some form of "positive contact?"

Comments: _____

_____

_____

Power to Influence Approach

_____ The student is beyond the effects of the _Influence Approach_; therefore, did the teacher use the _Power Approach_?

Check which of the following components of the _Power Approach_ the teacher employed:

_____ Teacher approached from the front

_____ Teacher made eye contact

_____ Teacher's breathing was shallow and high

_____ Teacher stood closely, maybe touching the student

_____ Teacher was verbal, perhaps with loud voice

Seatwork Checklist

_____ Once the student was in a Neutral state, did the teacher switch to the *Influence Approach?*

Check which components of the *Influence Approach* the teacher employed.

    _____ Teacher at the student's side

    _____ Teacher looked at the work on the student's desk

    _____ Teacher's breathing was low and full

    _____ The teacher either used non-verbal communication or whispered

Vacuum Pause:

_____ Did the teacher intervene with the student at the student's vacuum pause so that the student was automatically in the Neutral mental state; and, therefore, the teacher was able to immediately go to the *Influence Approach*?

Comments: _____

_____

_____

_____

OFF/Neutral/ON Refinements

Teacher has some of the pupils categorized into three groups:

_____ Group H = those the teacher helps

_____ Group H & M = those the teacher both helps and manages

_____ Group M = those the teacher mainly manages

Dot-to-Dot:

_____ Did the teacher prioritize her time and energy so that any optional teacher time was spent with Groups H and H & M?

_____ When the teacher assisted the Group H & M students, did their ON task behavior improve?

_____ Did the teacher distinguish between Group M students who were interfering with others' work and those who were OFF task but not interfering with others' learning? If the teacher intervened with the former and not the latter (unless the teacher had time), then the teacher prioritized.

Seatwork Checklist

Two Stage Exiting:

_____ When a student has been ON task for at least two breaths, did the teacher slowly posture her body so that the teacher was standing upright and next to the student?

_____ In order not to elicit an interchange between the student and teacher, did the teacher keep her eyes on the student's work?

_____ Did the teacher slowly and gradually step back from the student so that the student couldn't easily see the teacher leaving?

_____ Did the teacher peripherally watch the student to make sure the pupil remained ON task independent of the teacher?

_____ Did the teacher move about the room with this targeted student in mind? The purpose is to increase the distance from which the teacher can influence the student to remain ON task. Once the initial contact between the teacher and student has resulted in the student being ON task, then often a look from the teacher will remind the student to stay ON task.

Comments: _____

_____

Positive Reinforcement: One-on-One

_____ Did the teacher put a marginal student ON task?

_____ Did the teacher reinforce the student's ON task behavior while the student was still on task but starting to fade from concentration?

Check which of the following positive reinforcement techniques were employed:

_____ Verbal communication

_____ Non-verbal communication

_____ Verbal and non-verbal communication

Comments: _____

_____

Positive Reinforcement: Group Feedback

_____ Did the teacher have a silent visual feedback system to communicate to the class how they were doing?

_____ Did the teacher employ the silent feedback system of *Positive Reinforcement*? In other words, did the teacher stroke the class as they neared the end of their concentration and did this good timing increase the students' ON task behavior?

Seatwork Checklist

3 Before Me

_____ Did the teacher have a poster explaining the system?

_____ When a teacher was working with a student and another student approached her, did the teacher use a non-verbal signal to ask if the approaching student had sought the information the student wanted from the other sources?

_____ Did the student approach the teacher for information using the non-verbal signal to communicate that he had sought the information from other sources?

Comments: _____

_____

_____

Phantom Hand

_____ Did the teacher do the following while working with a marginal student who was ON task?

    _____ Keep her torso still, especially her feet

    _____ Look at the student's work

    _____ Increase Touch by

        _____ Original touch with fingers spread

        _____ Initial increase

        _____ Additional increase

    _____ Decrease Touch by

        _____ Decreasing from the additional pressure back to the initial increase of contact

        _____ Decrease from the initial increase back to the original touch

        _____ Gradually lift hand from original touch to barely touching

    _____ Lift Off by

        _____ Gradually lift hand from barely touching to being 1/2 inch from contact

        _____ Gradually lift hand from 1/2 inch to a foot away from point of contact

        _____ Gradually drop hand to teacher's side

    _____ Exiting by

        _____ Slowly exiting so the student cannot easily see the teacher

Comments: _____

_____

ENVoY—An Alternative to Clinical Supervision
The Teaching of the Skill, Not Just the Practice

*"We cannot empower with power;
We empower with influence."*

Too often in education we provide opportunities for the practice before students comprehend the skill. For example, we do "mental math" in the classroom by saying, "The bus picked up ten people at the first stop, doubled the number at the next stop and, at the third stop, one more person got on. At the fourth stop, one-third of the people got off. How many people are still on the bus?" There is no question that those students who can do mental math are improving from this activity, but the exercise did nothing to assist those students who don't know how to do the skill. It is the debriefing of the problem on the board, or better yet, at the students' individual desks re-enacting the scene with real objects which would help these students actually learn the skill.

Likewise, we can't expect teachers to automatically learn from experience; wisdom is the sharing of our collective reflection on experiences. This is what ENVoY is: a gathering of strategies and patterns of what we do on those days when we are ON. ENVoY can be used by administrators and staff development executives as an aid in the teaching of classroom management skills. The second half of this book provides the practice of those skills.

ENVoY is a manual intended for professional growth. It can be used as an alternative to clinical supervision when assessing classroom management. ENVoY's design dovetails nicely into those school systems which have reached the level of professionalism where the teachers can communicate their professional goals for the year with their administrators. The process might be:

- Select phase(s) for improvement
  - select specific ENVoY skills
- Select dates for completion of
  - self form(s)
  - observer form(s)
- Final assessment

ENVoY fosters professional development through voluntary collaboration and peer coaching. Final assessment can be done by colleagues or administrators.

ENVoY can be employed in an involuntary manner by directing a teacher to improve in one or more of the four phases of the lesson. If, as an administrator, you are forced to use this involuntary usage of ENVoY, keep in mind the techniques we covered in the *Power to Influence* skillsheet. It is okay to use POWER to shake up a person (teacher or student), but be careful not to get caught in the "authority" mode. If you get the person's attention (remember Samuel the mule), switch to the *Influence Approach* as soon as you are able. A goalsetting sheet is offered for your consideration.

ENVoY—An Alternative to Clinical Supervision

ENVoY Goal Setting and Self Assessment Sheet

Name _____   Time Period _____

School _____   Subject/Grade Level _____

The following are the four phases of a lesson. Using the following codes, assess your skill level on some or all of the ENVoY 31 skills.

A = Aware of; the name of the skill is familiar.
U = Understand some or all of the components of the skill.
D = Doing the skill periodically.
H = Habit; most of the time I do the skill automatically.

Indicate which skills you want to focus on as the classroom management component of your professional development by placing an F (Focus) in front of three to ten skills. Complete page 268 with these skills.

Getting Their Attention

____ Freeze Body (p10)
____ ABOVE (Pause) Whisper (p18)
____ Freeze Body Refinements (p44)
____ Opening Visual Instructions (p48)
____ Incomplete Sentences (p52)
____ Positive Comments (p56)
____ Decontaminating the Classroom (p58)
____ Break & Breathe (p62)
____ Yellow Light (p66)

Teaching

____ Raise Your Hand vs. Speak Out (p22)
____ Raise Your Hand vs. Speak Out
      Refinements (p72)
____ Increasing Non-verbal Signals (p78)
____ Overlap (p82)
____ Opposite Side of the Room (p86)
____ Verbal Rapport w/ Hard to Reach (p88)
____ Use Action Words Last (p94)

Transition to Seatwork

____ Exit Directions (p28)
____ Most Important Twenty Seconds (p32)
____ Exit Direction Refinements (p102)
____ Advanced Exit Directions (p106)
      Maintaining the Productive Atmosphere:
____ Private Voice (p110)
____ Walking Speed (p112)
____ Mini MITS (p114)

Seatwork

____ OFF/Neutral/ON (p34)
____ Influence Approach (p38)
____ Power to Influence Approach (p122)
____ OFF/Neutral/ON Refinements (p132)
      Positive Reinforcement:
____ One-on-One (p138)
____ Group Feedback (p142)
____ 3 Before Me (p146)
____ Phantom Hand (p148)

Meet with your principal and fill out page 268 to complete your plan of implementation.

ENVoY – An Alternative to Clinical Supervision
Plan of Implementation

It would be wise to include the following: when the teacher will be doing each Self Form, when and by whom the Peer Form will be done, who will be doing the Final Assessment and what it will consist of.

SKILLS	SELF FORM Chapters 1-5 (by when)	PEER FORM Chapters 6-10 (by when)	FINAL ASSESSMENT Chapters 6-10 (by whom/when; use Peer Form)
_____	_____	_____	_____
_____	_____	_____	_____
_____	_____	_____	_____
_____	_____	_____	_____
_____	_____	_____	_____
_____	_____	_____	_____
_____	_____	_____	_____
_____	_____	_____	_____
_____	_____	_____	_____
_____	_____	_____	_____

Additional aspects of plan:

_____

_____

_____

_____

Teacher's Name	Evaluator's Name
Teacher's Signature	Evaluator's Signature
	Evaluator's Position
School/District	Evaluator's Full Address

Inservice Offerings

*"Habit is habit, and not to be flung out the window by any man
but coaxed downstairs a step at a time."*
Mark Twain

Often the restructuring of a school's preventive disciplinary program is like a home remodeling project; it is done in stages. All of the Michael Grinder & Associates' ENVoY inservices have the same goal: to train entire staffs and resident coaches in The Seven Gems. The coaches would continue to assist their colleagues with their refinement of these skills.

It takes a minimum of three days to train the staff. This can be done either during the school year or during vacation. It takes one week during the school year to train resident coaches. A maximum of five schools select two teachers to attend the week-long coaches' training. Ideally, the five schools would be within a 30 minute drive from each other.

Resident Coach Trainee

The following is a list of characteristics of the ideal coach trainee. You will know best which of these descriptions are more important than others for your school program. Upon request, assistance will be given in the selection of the resident coaches during staff trainings as requested.

- Receptive—is accepted and respected by the staff. Sometimes it is smart to select coaches who would have the widest range of acceptance by the teachers.

- Perceptive—can recognize patterns between the teacher's behaviors, especially non-verbal behaviors and how his or her class responds to those behaviors.

- Feedback—can give feedback that is non-judgmental and is respectful of the teacher's beliefs and values by couching the feedback wording under an umbrella that motivates the teacher as a professional.

- Longevity—the coach trainee will be teaching within the district for a number of years so the time and money spent is most beneficial.

A description of the goals for subsequent years' inservice programs will be broached as training warrants.

ENVoY, like all models of classroom management, is intended to help learning occur. Therefore, the above formats can be modified to meet the needs of your particular educational setting.

ENVoY Quotes

Effective management is being "quiet as a _ _ _ _ _."   Pg. 1

We are inadvertently in love with the Influence of Power and we need to be in love with the Power of Influence.   Pg. 2

By employing the full range of non-verbal skills of ENVoY, we can learn to manage with finesse and thus nurture the powerful relationships of influence with students. Barbara Lawson   Pg. 3

From whence cometh professional wisdom? From our collective insightful reflection on experience.   Pg. 3

Visiting our colleague's room will allow us to see the process forest from the content trees.   Pg. 3

A road sign doesn't have to have been to a destination in order to direct someone there.   Pg. 5

The systematic use of non-verbal signals is the essence of masterful communication.   Pg. 12

The single most powerful non-verbal skill is the P A U S E.   Pg. 12

Teachers are seasonal workers whose tongues get tired and wear out before any other part of their body.   Pg. 29

A child will get our attention; the question of whether it is positive or negative is based on how soon and often we give it.   Pgs. 39 & 138

Getting a class under way is much like having a ship leave a dock—the better the timing with the ebb and flow, the easier the voyage.   Pg. 43

We are never paid to feel when we do management.   Pg. 43

Don't hunt field mice with elephant guns.   Pg. 43

The productivity of seatwork is a by-product of how we set sail as we leave the harbor of teaching and navigate into seatwork.   Pg. 99

One of the main purposes of ENVoY is to switch our profession from one of Power management to management by Influence.   Pg. 99

When teachers use power to put students ON task, the instructors handcuff themselves by being the motivator for the student's compliant behavior. When teachers use the methods of influence, we are getting the pupils to think they are the ones motivating themselves.   Pg. 119

Education believes that there is actually a "system solution" to our classroom ailments; hence, the perennial journey to a pedagogical mecca turns out to be just another short-lived educational fad. "Systems" won't affect the drop-out population...relationships do.   Pg. 119

The issue of curriculum for the kinesthetic learner is currently outside the scope of school. These students are disenfranchised because they cannot get their strokes from academic success. As educators, our option is to establish relationships.   Pg. 120

The extreme right-brain kinesthetic student is a member of the ESP Club = Earth as a Second Planet.   Pg. 125

ENVoY is a vehicle to shift educators from seeing themselves as bastions of power to instruments of influence.   Pg. 155

We need to elevate ourselves from within...we need systems which set aside time and prioritize money to enable us to profit from the wealth of abilities that lie in insular classrooms. It is only through sharing and supporting processes that the collective wisdom of the staff emerges.   Pg. 155

The classroom can be viewed with educational binoculars. ENVoY focuses on the management aspects of the learning environment. Equally important is the other educational tube--curriculum. A teacher can only be a successful manager if he or she can manage the student(s) into work where the student is successful.   Pg. 155

An ENVoY peer supports colleagues to professionally grow and lets them decide in which area.   Pg. 159

ENVoY is intended to be an educational smorgasbord with each reader selecting only those items that match the teacher's palate.   Pg. 223

The influence of power is short-lived while the power of influence is endless.   Pg. 223

Our profession needs teachers with big hearts who also know how to take care of themselves. The more realistically we can view our range of influence, the more we take pride in what we can do, resulting in our having higher motivation.   Pgs. 232 & 134

Our profession is famous for doing things because of a philosophical consideration we believe in, even if it is less than effective use of our time and energy.   Pg. 233

We cannot empower with power; we empower with influence.   Pg. 266

Index

The following index is for Chapters One through Five and the Introduction to Peer Forms. When a skill appears on a page other than mentioned in the Table of Contents, it will be listed here. Because the ten gem skills are so omnipresent, they will not be listed.

© 1993 Michael Grinder & Associates, ENVoY 05 (360) 687-3238; FAX (360) 687-0595; www.michaelgrinder.com

Management Trilogy

After 17 years of teaching experience on three levels of education, Michael visited 6,000 classrooms. He wanted to find out, "What do the most effective teachers have in common?" From these visitations, he identified the patterns that were almost universally seen in high-quality learning environments. He formulated what he observed into clear and easily learned management strategies, sorted them into three major categories, and published the results in this trilogy:

- *A Cat In The Dog House*—How to establish relationships with the hard-to-reach students.
- *ENVoY*—How to preserve the relationships while managing.
- *A Healthy Classroom*—How to utilize relationships between the students—group dynamics.

Successful management is based on a positive working relationship between the teacher and the students. Michael's products and trainings are based on the following axiom:

We are inadvertently in love with the influence of Power

We need to be in love with the power of Influence.

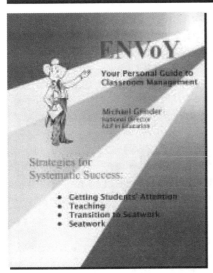

ENVoY: Your Personal Guide to Classroom Management

ENVoY is the flagship of the Michael Grinder and Associates Classroom Management Trilogy.

Seven Gems

ENVoY is a collection of 31 classroom management techniques that every teacher needs—techniques you can pull out of your "toolbox" the minute you most need them. Chapter One is a summary of the seven techniques that teachers have told us, time and again, are the quickest to get results and the easiest to use.

Shifting from Power to Influence

ENVoY gives educators specific ways to manage from influence instead of power. Use ENVoY with other instructors from your school to bring out the strengths in all and create a vibrant, dynamic learning community. Elevate from within… ENVoY creates systems that enable you to profit from the wealth of abilities your school holds. It is only through sharing and supporting one another that the collective wisdom of the staff emerges.

Complete System

Research shows that peer coaching is the single fastest way to increase professional growth. This book makes it easy to do peer coaching on the 31 skills by including worksheets that can be used alone or with a peer. Also included is an inventory of teacher management strengths. By completing this inventory as a team, a teacher and principal can quickly determine the focuses for professional development.

Title

The unusual spelling of our title stands for Educational Non Verbal Yardsticks, with a small "o" added to create the word *envoy*. The symbol for our envoy, a mouse, reminds us throughout the book of tips such as "when managing, be quiet as a _ _ _ _ _." Our envoy communicates the educational culture's best secrets both to newcomers and to established members of the culture. The second reason why the mouse is our symbol is because the computer mouse allows us to work with speed and efficiency. We want to manage with speed and efficiency so we can get back to why we became a teacher—to help students learn.

New Teachers

In spite of their importance, the ENVoY techniques are rarely taught in teacher preparation programs. The number one reason that new teachers leave our profession is a lack of training in effective classroom management. Research has shown that ENVoY techniques allow new teachers to concentrate on teaching.

$29.95

The Seven Gems DVD: Companion to ENVoY

The top Seven Gems of classroom management are presented in this DVD. The footage is from a training seminar so that you receive the actual sense of learning the skill. The video demonstrates the techniques used to get the compliance from the students while preserving the relationship with the pupils. $49.95 (Also available in VHS format while supplies last.) (See the Seven Gems In-service Kit for school or district purchase.)

ENVoY Book and The Seven Gems DVD

A special package of Michael Grinder's best selling work at a great price! Get the package of the ENVoY book and the Seven Gems DVD for $69.95—a savings of $9.95.

The Seven Gems In-service Kit: Companion to ENVoY

(Video, 60 Transparencies, 120-page Manual)

The Kit is intended for schools, staff development and training institutes. The Kit is designed for each of the *7 Gems* to be shown from the video and then the tape is stopped and a series of transparencies allows the educators watching to practice the practical skills. The Presenter Guide indicates what to say while showing the transparencies and answers any questions that may arise. $295.00

Seven Gems Pamphlets

The very best skills from *ENVoY* are known as the Seven Gems. Each pamphlet is devoted to one of the seven skills. The size allows the recipient to have a quick understanding of a practical skill. The set is ideal for giving to an educator who isn't quite ready to purchase a book. Set of 7: $5.00

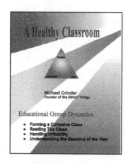

A Healthy Classroom

This book sheds light on the most difficult management situations that teachers face—group dynamics. Only by understanding the sophisticated patterns that affect both the individual pupil and the class as a whole can the educator have all the possible management choices. This seminal work includes: group formation and cohesiveness, reading the class, identifying and utilizing the leadership, recognizing and adjusting to the seasons of the year, the stages a group goes through and how each stage warrants different responses from the teacher. A special section is devoted to fostering group health. Book comes with rubrics, Post-its and screen savers. Book: $34.95

A Cat in the Dog House

ENVoY has struck a nerve in the educational community around the world. The book has been translated into six languages. The purpose of the ENVoY program is to preserve relationships with students during management.

The demographics of the classroom have changed. Increasingly, students seem to resist the teacher's attempts to form a relationship. Michael's *A Cat in the Dog House* addresses this dilemma and retools educators with successful strategies to form working relationships with these hard-to-reach students. Book: Visit www.michaelgrinder.com for announcement of publication. In the meantime we recommend Michael's book, *Charisma—The Art of Relationships*, which describes relationships with adults.

Charisma—The Art of Relationships

Why are some people easy to influence and work with and others are not? *Charisma—The Art of Relationships* delightfully answers this question and instructs how to increase your charisma. Using the analogy of house pets, this work provides methods to help you:

- Understand and accept yourself and others
- Separate your and others' intention from actions
- Interpret your and others' behaviors more accurately
- Increase resolving conflicts and knowing which conflicts not to try to resolve
- Improve your leadership skills and manage difficult personalities

The concepts are highlighted with icons in the margins indicating that a worksheet has been developed to practice the skill. Over 100 worksheets have been created which are available free at www.michaelgrinder.com.

This paperback book is 5½" x 8½" with 144 pages. Its compact size allows the reader to carry it anywhere. Book: $11.95.

Charisma Worksheets and Screen Savers

We are all very busy and yet want to continue to professionally grow. Screen savers address this need. When our computers are at rest, the concepts appear on the screen with an attractive background. The page reference is listed to encourage us to further extend our learning. Free downloads are available from the MGA website: www. michaelgrinder.com.

Charisma—The Art of Relationships

Live from London, DVD and Audio Album

Spend 1-1/2 hours with Michael as he entertainingly applies his cat and dog analogy to a wide array of applications. Topics include raising teenagers, understanding how to manage difficult personalities, increasing the efficiency of committee meetings and developing presentation skills. Michael's engaging style, humorous anecdotes and poignant insights will have you both laughing and reflecting at the same time. DVD & Audio Album: $49.95. (Album includes a Bonus CD of Charisma Worksheets and Screen Savers.) Also sold separately. DVD: $39.95; Audio CD: $19.95.

Righting the Educational Conveyor Belt

Successful teachers have a variety of management strategies and instructional techniques. *Righting the Educational Conveyor Belt* is the curriculum companion to the ENVoY Trilogy. *Righting the Educational Conveyor Belt* assists the teacher in identifying and utilizing students' learning styles, establishing patterns for their long term memory and increasing the pupils' visual capacity for test taking. All concepts are explained in practical terms and easily implemented. While immediately usable for all grade levels, the book directly assists "kids at risk." Book: $23.95

Audio CDs

As much as we all enjoy DVD, many of us find that our driving time is the occasion for professional development. Three Educational CDs on the At-risk Population, Building Relationships and Avoiding Escalations & Confrontations. These are live recordings from Michael presenting at a national conference. $19.95

For administrators: The Fundamentals of Group Dynamics (3 CDs) on How Not to Get Shot!, Handling Attacks and Overcoming Resistance. $59.95

The Elusive Obvious (The Science of Non Verbal Communication)

80–90% of all communication is nonverbal. Michael's delineation of the 21 patterns of what one can do with one's eyes, voice, body (including gestures and location) and breathing is a major breakthrough. Even more amazing is the fact that the patterns are cross-culturally accurate. Included is a DVD of these 21 nonverbal patterns and How Not to Get Shot! This DVD is designed to teach people how to deliver volatile information while preserving the relationship. Book & DVD: $89.95

First Days of School by Harry Wong

The First Days of School is for new and veteran teachers from kindergarten to college. You will learn about management, teaching for mastery and to standards, and creating positive expectations. A graphic layout, with 302 photos and illustrations, is partnered with text that flows smooth as silk. This revised and updated version includes a 35 minute bonus multimedia enhanced CD. Book plus CD: $29.95

A Framework for Understanding Poverty by Ruby Payne

This is a seminal work for teachers and professionals who work and assist people from poverty. In a non-judgmental manner, Dr. Payne delineates the differences between socio- economic classes. The book shifts educators to a more meaningful understanding of how to offer, without imposing, assistance to students from poverty. Book: $22.00

Yacker Tracker

This device provides feedback to the class on their noise level. The traffic light is computerized with adjustable sound level meter. Green light stays lit until noise in room goes above set level, then a flashing yellow light comes on as a warning. When sound level reaches 20 decibels above set level, a red light and (optional) siren sounds. $49.95

Teach Timer

This mechanism indicates the amount of time remaining for a task. An indispensable "time management tool" for teachers and trainers. Teach timers are specifically designed to use in cooperative leaning groups, timing tests, reading assignments, science experiments or any other classroom or school activity. $45.00

Thinklers by Kevin Brougher

Want to warm up your students' brains? Thinklers has over 300 pages with thousands of thinklers as well as Commonyms and Twosome puzzles. Thinklers involve a few words spelled either upwards, backwards, to the left or right, up or down, spelled in different sizes or positions AND after careful study one will find an altogether different meaning. This resource is ideal for an "Opening Visual Instruction." (See page 48.) Book: $16.50

Mentoring Matters by Wellman and Lipton

An invaluable reference for mentors of beginning teachers, this guide offers structures, strategies and tools for developing expertise in teaching. Sections include specific information about the mentor's role, the needs of beginning teachers and the attributes of effective mentor-protégé relationships. Tips for maximizing time and attention, an extensive resource section and blackline masters to support developmental interactions make this book a must-have for mentors. Book: $24.95

Amazing Face Reading

Face reading is a means to a deeper communication with every person you meet. Fulfer takes this art/science out of the realm of the mysterious and into a hands-on method of learning. The most comprehensive, easy-to-use book of Face Reading available today. Amazing Face Reading is organized in an encyclopedic format and superbly illustrated. It takes you through faces, top to bottom, detail to gestalt, gesture to metaphoric meaning. This how-to guide is so easy to use that you can begin to read faces before you finish the book. $17.95

Tear Soup by Pat Schweibert, Chuck DeKlyen, Pat Schwiebert

Tear Soup, a recipe for healing after loss, is a family story book. It recognizes and reinforces the fact that every member of the family from the youngest to the oldest will grieve in their own way. Taking their own time and in doing so, find those things which help them best. Essentially, we each make our own batch of Tear Soup when we grieve the loss of someone we love or for any major change in our lives. By emphasizing the individual process of bereavement by making soup, Grandy's brings a warm and comfortable feeling to an otherwise difficult subject matter for many individuals. Book: $19.95

Teaching with Love and Logic

Do you find yourself facing a variety of classroom situations never covered in your initial training? This valuable resource will help you increase your skills, enhance your professional development, and maximize learning time in your classroom.

Discover why Love and Logic works in the school environment, and understand the psychological reasons for its effectiveness. Jim Fay and David Funk's truly positive approach and time-tested ideas and strategies will empower teachers to effectively manage classroom dynamics while bringing the joy back to teaching. Book: $17.95

Parenting with Love and Logic

You'll raise children who are self-confident, motivated, and ready for the real world with this win-win approach to parenting. Your children will win because they'll learn to solve their own problems while gaining the confidence they need to meet life's challenges. And, you'll win because you'll establish healthy control without resorting to anger, threats, nagging, or exhausting power struggles. *Parenting with Love and Logic* puts the fun back into parenting! Book: $24.95

New Management Handbook by Rick Morris

Do you find that you love to teach but the paperwork kills you? Now you can learn the simple system that is revolutionizing the elementary classroom. Based upon his incredibly successful New Management seminar series, the New Management Handbook is a step-by-step guide that will unleash the dynamic power of Rick Morris's system of student management, motivation and involvement. In just 10 easy lessons, you'll find everything you need to create a happier, more productive classroom and enable yourself to become a more effective teacher. Book: $20.00

Classroom Magic by Linda Lloyd

This skillfully crafted workbook with 38 weeks of lesson plans shows teachers and parents advanced communication techniques targeted for behavior and learning. Learn specific methods to enhance perception in your students, speak directly to the unconscious mind, deal effectively with special learners, promote profound and lasting behavioral change, and have more fun while teaching! Practical and valuable for classroom or home schooling and adaptable for all ages. Book: $17.95

Rediscover The Joy of Learning by Don Blackerby

This book is in three major sections: Academic Skills for Students; Tips for Parents, Teachers and Counselors, and; Learning Disabilities (primarily Attention Deficit Disorder or ADD). The book is in a handbook format, very easy to read and apply. Anybody can use the book without any specialized training. Specifically designed for educators who work one on one, for example, special education teachers. To date, it has been used by students of all ages—grade school to college and adults in corporate learning centers, adults wishing to go back to school, teachers at all levels, and parents and counselors of students who struggle in school. Book: $24.95

My Baby Can Talk, Doug and Kathleen Waidhofer

My Baby Can Talk™ is a series of products developed to teach babies to talk with their hands before they can speak. Included in this series of products are videos, board books and flashcards. The first video released by Baby Hands Productions is My Baby Can Talk™ - First Signs. We plan to produce at least four more videos with each video teaching twenty words that are most relevant for and most loved by young babies. Each video will have a corresponding board book and set of flashcards that represent the same words taught in the video. Board books and flashcards are resources that can be purchased separately and used to reinforce the signs taught in each video. Products listed and sold at ww.mybabycantalk.com

Ungame: Rhea Zakich

The Ungame is a board game that, as the name implies, is not intended for competition for but communication. The author, at one time in her life, was unable to talk. After meals of mostly silence, she wrote cards with questions on them and placed them at her family's plates. The circle of communication was revived. In time she became so comfortable with her temporary affliction that she resumed giving dinner parties. Her guests had such a great time that they encouraged her to publish the product; hence, the board game. The board game comes with generic questions. The two decks we carry are for couples and for family. Couples Cards: $9.00; Family Cards: $9.00

www.michaelgrinder.com

Visit our website for:

• free downloadable screen savers for *Charisma—The Art of Relationships* and *A Healthy Classroom*.

• free downloadable worksheets

• schedule of Michael's classes

• list of recognized ENVoY trainers and their class schedules

• sign up for free email quote of the day

• latest announcements

• research on ENVoY

• additional products

MGA PRODUCT ORDER FORM

Title	Unit Price	Quantity	Total
ENVoY by Michael Grinder			
ENVoY: Your Personal Guide to Classroom Management. Michael Grinder. Book. 40% discount on 10 or more	29.95		
ENVoY Seven Gems DVD, Michael Grinder	49.95		
ENVoY Book and Seven Gems DVD, Michael Grinder	69.95		
ENVoY Seven Gems Pamphlets (set of 7). Michael Grinder 10% discount on orders of 10 to 19; 20% discount on orders of 20 or more.	5.00		
ENVoY The Seven Gems In-service Kit, Michael Grinder	295.00		
Charisma by Michael Grinder			
Charisma—The Art of Relationships, Michael Grinder. Book. 10% discount on orders of 10 to 19; 20% discount on orders of 20 or more.	11.95		
Charisma—The Art of Relationships, Live from London, Michael Grinder. DVD	39.95		
Charisma—The Art of Relationships, Live from London, Michael Grinder. Audio CD	19.95		
Charisma—The Art of Relationships, Live from London, Michael Grinder. DVD & Audio Album (with Bonus CD of Worksheets and Screen Savers)	49.95		
Charisma—The Art of Relationships. Cat & Dog Profile	7.50		
A Cat in the Dog House, Michael Grinder (forthcoming book)	*		
Other Products by Michael Grinder			
The Elusive Obvious (The Science of Non Verbal Communication): Vignettes of How Not to Get Shot! and Pentimento plus DVD, Michael Grinder	89.95		
How Not to Get Shot! and Pentimento, DVD, Michael Grinder	49.95		
Fundamentals of Group Dynamics (3 CDs): How Not to Get Shot!, Handling Attacks, Overcoming Resistance, Michael Grinder	59.95		
A Healthy Classroom, Michael Grinder 40% discount on 10 or more	34.95		
Righting The Educational Conveyor Belt, Michael Grinder 40% discount on 10 or more	23.95		
Educational (3) CDs on the At-risk, Building Relationships, Avoiding Escalations & Confrontations, Michael Grinder	19.95		

*Check www.michaelgrinder.com for availability and price

Rev. 06/07

Other Educational Products

Classroom Magic, Linda Lloyd NLP for elementary teachers; excellent week-by-week plan.	17.95		
First Days of School, Harry Wong	29.95		
Mentoring Matters, Laura Lipton & Bruce Wellman	24.95		
New Management Handbook, Rick Morris	20.00		
Poverty: A Framework for Understanding and Working With Students and Adults from Poverty, Ruby Payne, Ph.D.	22.00		
Rediscover the Joy of Learning, Don A. Blackerby, Ph.D. A hand book for teachers, counselors and parents of struggling students.	24.95		
Teaching with Love and Logic. Book. Jim Fay and David Funk.	17.95		
Thinklers, Kevin Brougher	16.50		
Teach Timer	45.00		
Yacker Tracker	49.95		

Other Corporate Products

Amazing Face Reading, Mac Fulfer	17.95		
Presenter's Field Guide, R. Garmston	32.95		
You Just Don't Understand, Deborah Tannen. Men and women conversation styles.	14.00		

Other Home Products

Parenting with Love and Logic. Foster Cline, M.D. and Jim Fay.	24.95		
Tear Soup; A Recipe For Healing After Loss, P. Schwiebert & C. DeKlyen	19.95		
The Ungame Couples Cards. Great conversation starters.	9.00		
The Ungame Family Cards	9.00		
SUBTOTAL			
Shipping & Handling (does not apply to people purchasing in training room) ($25.00 or less, add $7.00) ($25.01 to $50, add $8.00) ($50.01 to $100, add $9.00) ($100.01 or more = cost of shipping)			
Washington residents add 7.7% sales tax			
TOTAL			

All prices subject to change.

Name: _____ Phone _____

Address: _____

City: _____ State: _____ Zip _____

Pymnt Method: ❑Check enc.❑ PO #_____. Credit Card: ❑VISA. ❑MasterCard. Exp. Date ____

Card No. _____ Signature: _____

Michael Grinder & Associates · 16303 N.E. 259th Street · Battle Ground, WA 98604
Phone: (360) 687-3238 · Fax (360) 687-0595
Website: www.michaelgrinder.com

Rev. 06/07